BKPM

BARE KNUCKLED
PROJECT MANAGEMENT

HOW TO SUCCEED AT EVERY PROJECT

BY TONY GRUEBL & JEFF WELCH

WITH MICHAEL DOBSON
ART BY BARTLEY COLLART

GAMEPLAN PRESS

GAMEPLAN PRESS

910 South George Mason Drive
Arlington, Virginia 22204
www.gameplanpress.com

Artwork and illustrations are by Bartley Collart except as noted in "Photo and Image Credits" beginning on page 211.

ISBN-13 978-061581-3943
ISBN-10 0615813941

Printed in the United States of America

10 9 8 7 6 5 4 3 2 1

Table of Contents

Foreword 3

Chapter 1: Projects in Crisis 11

Chapter 2: The Bare-Knuckled Project Manager......... 23

Chapter 3: The Three-Sided Table................................. 35

Chapter 4: No Bullshit Project Management................. 65

Chapter 5: Why Projects Fail — and How BKPM
Prevents It 91

Chapter 6: Becoming a Bare-Knuckled Project Manager
....109

Chapter 7: Conflict and Communications................... 133

Chapter 8: The Kranz Dictum 153

Chapter 9: The Next Bout................................ 173

Chapter 10: Transforming the Project — and the
Organization 193

Glossary.. 205

Bibliography.. 209

Photo and Image Credits................................ 211

Acknowledgements....................................... 213

About the Authors.................................... 215

Foreword

IN MARCH 2009, the telephone rang. I answered. "Tony
Gruebl."

"Hey, Tony. It's Jeff." Jeff Welch was my client, working
for a government services division of a well-known global
provider of IT and strategic business process outsourcing
services.

I was surprised to hear from him. "I thought you were in
Alabama, working on that Air Force project," I said.

"I am in Alabama. That's why I'm calling. I just got out of
some meetings. It's bad — really bad. Got a few minutes?"

I did. Jeff's company used me as their go-to project
manager for non-standard (read: difficult) projects, ever since
I'd handled a large and risky LMS system deployment for
them about five years ago. And I knew Jeff wasn't the kind of
guy to hit the alarm over nothing.

In retrospect, Jeff's call really wasn't that much of a
surprise. I'd worked with them through the bid and award
process, so I knew the situation. I also knew they'd hired a
seasoned project manager with a military background to be

their on-site PM for the project. I was supposed to provide coaching and support for that project manager, but he'd been ignoring me ever since the contract had been awarded. I could sense something was — well, perhaps not wrong, but definitely a bit off.

Jeff quickly set me straight. "You wouldn't believe what's going on down here. I've never seen such a mess. To start, I think I'm going to need to fire the project manager. No, strike that. I know I'm going to need to fire the PM."

That surprised me. "You mean that guy you moved down from Virginia? I thought he was really well qualified. He seemed like a strong project leader."

"Well, that's what we thought," Jeff said. "You wouldn't believe the personal issues this guy is dealing with. It has him all screwed up. That's what my meetings started to be about. Then I started digging beyond the PM's personal issues and looked into the status reports, and they're completely wrong. Nothing on this project is as it's been reported. It's like you've been flying along for hours and suddenly realize that no one's in the cockpit! I have no idea where we are, where we've been, or where we're going. I've got to get a handle on this immediately!"

When the situation is this bad, you don't have any time to waste. "How about the onsite project team?" I asked. "How are they doing?

"They're the ones who brought the situation to my attention," Jeff said. "It's a good crew. They care about the project, and they understand the need for leadership — and leadership looks like it's gone AWOL."

In response to a few more questions, Jeff filled in the rest of the story. The team was following the original plan, but requirements were shifting without anyone making sure the project was aligned with the changing goals. "We might not be in too bad shape, but we might be totally screwed. I just don't know. I can't trust any of the data that's been coming from the project manager," he concluded.

I already had access to their accounting system because of the other projects I'd been managing for Jeff's company. "Get me permission to take a look at this project's financials, reports, communications, the current project plan, whatever you've got. I've got the original project plan I helped your guy create; that'll give me a baseline."

I could hear the relief in Jeff's voice. "Sounds good. Can you fly down next week? I need someone I can trust to peel back all the layers and find out exactly where we are, and I'm going to be knee-deep in personnel issues. I'm going to need a revised plan and detailed status before I have to explain to the colonel what's going on."

I knew how important this project was for Jeff's company. "I'll need to move some things around, but yes, I can help."

And so began a rescue effort. We quickly gained control over the project and made personnel changes, starting from the top. We had a few frank discussions with the colonel in charge and set up a workable action plan.

It took a year of constantly changing USAF personnel, evolving project requirements, and constant travel between Maryland and Alabama — but in the end, we got the job done.

You know this scenario – it happens far too often. If you haven't yet experienced a project in complete collapse, sooner or later you will. And when it does happen, and the only option is to succeed, conventional business practices and standard project management approaches aren't always up to the challenge.

The no-nonsense approach to getting the job done involves ruffling a few feathers, making some hard decisions, and speaking unpleasant truths to people who don't always want to hear bad news. I think of it as taking a bare-knuckled approach to project management, and that's what this book is all about.

You need to understand something. This isn't going to be a book of management platitudes, high-minded business practices, or a refinement of the standard project management materials taught in textbooks. It's about practicality and efficiency — keep what works and get rid of the rest. It's about what actually works in a wide variety of project types, project teams, and project owners.

And it will make project failure a thing of the past.

For me, living the idea of bare-knuckled project management is pretty much the way I am. I'm unconventional in my approach. I push back against business norms, especially when they aren't getting the job done. And I don't mind getting in the face of someone who's clearly out of touch with reality.

Frankly, I feel more comfortable articulating these ideas over a few beers in a Baltimore pub than in the pages of a book. (Not to mention that my colleagues didn't like my idea for the cover: me in a black leather jacket sitting astride a Harley.) On top of that, a lot of what I do instinctually has to be translated so that other people can do it to.

That's why I enlisted the help of three colleagues.

The first, Jeff Welch, you've already met. He's a technical solution architect who's been designing, building, and deploying information systems in government and commercial environments for nearly 25 years. Jeff is a master at taking complex information and converting it into something easily understandable. He has been integral in challenging me to extract and codify my knowledge and practices for this book, a process that involved more than a few beers and cocktail napkins. (Note: Jeff would like all tavern owners to provide whiteboards for their patrons.) Jeff and I together are the "soul" of the bare-knuckled project management process: this book is us.

Then there is Michael Dobson. I first met Michael Dobson through a mutual friend, and attended one of his project management workshops many years ago. I was struck by his clarity, practicality, and expertise, and I immediately went out and bought several of his books on project management.

(He's written ten of them — along with novels, business books, histories, and lots more, currently fifty books and counting.) Running a full-time business doesn't leave a lot of time for writing, and so I prevailed on Michael to take on this project as a third collaborator, taking the methodology Jeff and I developed and laying it out in written form, adding his expertise and insights to further flesh out the book.

I also enlisted the services of Bart Collart (L10.biz). Bart is a graphic artist and I emphasize artist. Jeff has been working with Bart for many years and was one of the first people he thought of when the need for an artist became self-evident. Pictures can communicate emotion and concepts non-verbally, which is important since many of the practices codified in this book focus on limbic brain conditioning: a level below the language centers of the brain.

Of course, many others have added their expertise and insight over the years. You'll find a list of acknowledgements at the very end, right before the author biographies.

What is this thing called Bare-Knuckled Project Management (BKPM for short)?

BKPM is first and foremost a mindset, a limbic conditioned response to produce a good outcome even when rational decision-making goes out the window because, as we just saw, sometimes we're thrown into a situation that's already out of control.

BKPM uses that limbic learning to force you to get your projects on the right track from the very first meeting. Maybe you'll be asked to step in when things are already bad, but when you're in charge from the beginning, you'll make sure these problems never happen in the first place.

If you've noticed that the mass production of traditional project managers isn't delivering the project results you need; if you've noticed that the most visible issue often becomes who to blame rather than how to fix it; if you've noticed that even smart and capable people all too often end up over their heads, then you'll benefit from this book.

My promise to you is that if you use the BKPM approach from the outset, project failure won't happen. That's a big promise, but as you'll see, it's one we'll keep.

But the book isn't the end of our conversation; it's simply the pre-read. To really experience what being a Bare-Knuckled Project Manager is all about, you and I need to talk. Give me a call at 443-725-5131 (my company, Think Systems, Inc.) or send me an email (tgruebl@thinksi.com).

I'm serious.

Call me.

Let's talk through it.

— Tony Gruebl

Projects in Crisis

The Lousy Track Record of Project Management

In 2012, "Project Shield," a $45 million US Department of Homeland Security technology initiative in Cook County, Illinois, had "equipment failures, poor planning, and poor training...as an integrated whole, the system was worthless." Contributing factors included lack of oversight, underestimation of complexity, and inefficient procurement practices. (Calleam Consulting, 2002)

In 2010, the US Navy's attempt to upgrade the Presidential helicopter fleet (Marine One), was cancelled after burning through $13 billion. Causes included underestimation of complexity, requirements instability, and ballooning scope.

Also in 2010, Microsoft's "Kin" phones were withdrawn from the market after only two months, after cutting the price in half failed to stimulate sales. Poor marketing, limited functionality, high operating costs, and a lack of executive support were credited. Losses were estimated in the region of $1 billion.

In 2009, the London Stock Exchange was forced to decommission its new trading platform after only two years in service and four years in development. System performance problems and unreliability were cited, with the root cause being an inappropriate choice of technologies.

Projects — large ones like these I've just cited, small ones, and everything in-between — are "failing" all around us.

How many of your projects get completed on time, on budget, and to spec? If the answer is "Not very many," you're not alone. According to the Standish Group's annual CHAOS Report, which surveys large corporate IT projects, nearly seventy-six percent of projects fail in part or in whole!

With a pathetic success rate of only 32%, it's no wonder that large projects are a nightmare for just about every organization. Even the small ones consume precious resources (e.g., time, money, people) that could have been used to make a business stronger. When you start to roll in such considerations as reputation, brand, and other market drivers, the cost of failed projects becomes truly mind-boggling. When this happens, there are no excuses. There's no place to hide... or at least there shouldn't be.

But there is an answer.

Figure 1-1. Project Failure Rates. 68% of projects fail in whole or in part. (Source: *CHAOS Summary 2009*, The Standish Group)

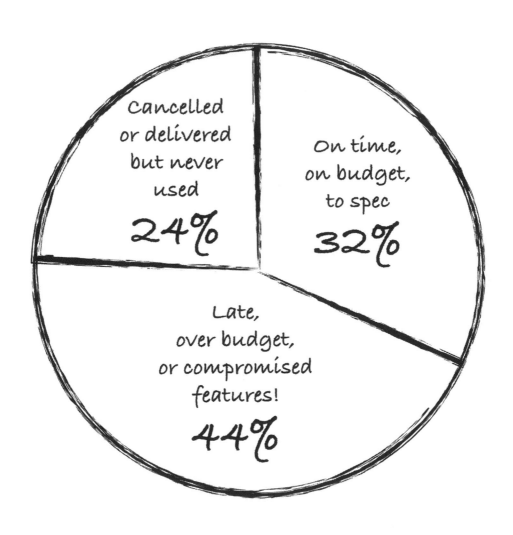

Why So Many Projects Fail

Just about every expert around has weighed in on the subject of why so many projects fail, and what it takes to make a project succeed. The Standish Group itself lists its "Chaos Ten" list of factors that makes projects successful.

Figure 1-2. The CHAOS Ten

The CHAOS Ten

1. User Involvement
2. Executive Support
3. Clear Business Objectives
4. Experienced Project Manager
5. Small Milestones
6. Firm Basic Requirements
7. Competent Staff
8. Proper Planning
9. Ownership
10. Other

Factors that make projects successful. Source: The Standish Group, 1999

Project Underperformance: The Elephant in the Room

Project failure is dramatic enough, but what about the cost of project underperformance? We've defined project failure as failing to meet one or more key goals, but even when the project achieves most or all of its requirements, it still may underperform.

Figure 1-3. Types of Project Underperformance

- Over budget, but complete
- Late, but complete
- Some functionality missing or overall functionality degraded (may also have issues with budget or schedule)
- Unplanned resources needed to reach the goal
- Other projects sacrificed or harmed to achieve the current project goal
- Unplanned and unexpected risks surprised the project team
- Project meets technical requirements but turns out not to meet real user needs
- Speed of change makes project obsolete even before it's completed

Sound familiar? If your reaction is, "Been there, done that," you're not alone.

Mere project survival usually isn't enough in today's fast-moving world. As famous quality guru W. Edwards Deming said, "Good enough isn't!" When your project technically succeeds, but fails to achieve operational greatness, efficiency, and excellence, or fails to correct a major organizational pain point or make the company better in some real, tangible way — those, too, are project failures of a different sort.

While some underperformance issues show up in the CHAOS statistics, many don't. That makes the numbers for project success even bleaker than they already appear.

Experienced — or Effective?

In spite of this bad news, we frequently give our most important projects to people whose claim to success is that they sat through training courses or got a PMP® (Project Management Professional) certificate from the Project Management Institute (PMI).

Is this really what you want? Or do you want your opportunities for organizational greatness to be in the hands of people who can lead, facilitate, negotiate, navigate, and above all, execute.

It's not enough to be an experienced project manager. You have to be an effective project manager. That takes the willingness to push hard and do what it takes — skills that aren't always welcome in a corporate environment.

Pushing hard isn't necessarily the same as being a hard-ass. There are any number of hard-ass project managers that drive their projects — right into the ground. There are also project managers who consistently make their deliverables — at the cost of long-term team effectiveness. They're like the kid who makes breakfast for Mother's Day and leaves the kitchen a wreck. Great on paper; horrible in practice. The right kind of effective blends the needs of the project with the needs and well-being of the operational teams that support them. That means not only success today, but also the capability for success tomorrow as well.

Projects, you see, have two defining characteristics. They are temporary and they are unique. The normal organization, by contrast, is designed for operational work — the regular and consistent activities we need to perform to keep the doors open.

Operational work has a number of advantages. You can design your organization to do it efficiently. You can train people in the processes and methods of handling the work. You can improve those processes and make them better. Just about every management system from TQM to Lean Six Sigma tells you how to improve your operational work.

But projects, by their very nature, break the mold. If you're lucky, the projects don't break the mold so much that they break down the operational efficiencies you have developed. But when you are trying to evolve your business or take risks in attempting to leverage new technologies, methods, or processes, conflict between projects and operations is simply going to be a fact of life.

Projects and Change

Projects are always about change. They deliver new systems and tools to improve the organization. They respond to challenges and crises. They force people outside their comfort zones and require new ways of thinking. And at the end of every project, the people and resources have to be folded back into the organization or sent on to new project challenges.

Whether your organization admits it or not, this makes a lot of people uncomfortable. A big project is like going off the high dive into uncharted water. You don't ever know what you're going to find. A big project forces change on departments and whole organizations. Everybody resists change to some extent; it's just human nature.

We all know about inertia — the tendency of a body at rest to stay at rest, and the tendency of a body once in motion to stay in motion. It's one of the fundamental principles of physics. It's also one of the fundamental rules of people and organizations. Whenever you try to push any part of the organization to move and change, inertia kicks in. It takes force — energy — to make it happen.

That's where the bare-knuckled project manager comes in.

Bare-Knuckle Boxing

JOHN L. SULLIVAN.
ALLEN & GINTER'S
RICHMOND. *Cigarettes* VIRGINIA.

What we think of as modern boxing evolved from ancient combat sports. In bare-knuckle fighting, as the name suggests, the fighters don't wear gloves or padding. Unlike a street fight, however, there are rules.

In England, bare-knuckle fighting became a recognized sport with a champion in the early 1700s. The first English champion, James Figg, gained the title in 1719 and held it until 1730.

Bare-knuckle bouts lasted much longer than modern boxing matches. One, in 1855, lasted for six hours and fifteen minutes. The last sanctioned match took place in 1899 between John L. Sullivan and Jake Kilrain, with Sullivan victorious.

After the Marquis of Queensberry developed modern boxing rules in 1867, bare-knuckle fighting slowly gave way to modern boxing. Some fighters adapted to the new system, including John L. Sullivan, who lost the battle to become the first heavyweight champion to Gentleman Jim Corbett in 1892.

There has been a revival of sorts for bare-knuckle boxing. In 2011, the first official bout since 1899 took place in Arizona.

When the Going Gets Tough, They Call In the Sons of Bitches

Admiral Ernest King, the Navy chief who won the Battle of the Atlantic in World War II, is supposed to have said, "When the going gets tough, they call in the sons of bitches."

Not all projects are wars, of course (though all wars are certainly projects). But some of the same skills and attitudes that make someone an effective military leader are also those that make for an effective project manager. The commitment to get the job done, the force of will to overcome resistance, and the foresight to manage problems and risks — these are just a few of the characteristics that matter.

It's not always necessary to be an actual son of a bitch. General George Patton was a remarkable and effective commander, but he also left a lot of collateral damage in his wake from his temper and his unwillingness to respect the organizational boundaries of his role. You can't be afraid to be a son of a bitch when the situation calls for it, but assertiveness, calm, and directness are often enough to carry the day.

In the movie *Pulp Fiction*, there's a scene where the two lead characters (John Travolta and Samuel L. Jackson) have a dead man in the back of their car, and call their boss Marcellus for help. Shortly, help arrives in the form of a man in a tuxedo. "I'm Winston Wolf. I solve problems," he says. Although Wolf never raises his voice, loses his temper, or acts with anything other than extreme politeness, he instantly takes command of the situation. To the two gangsters, the situation looks hopeless, but to Winston Wolf, it's all in a day's work.

Our name for this: Bare-Knuckled Project Management — BKPM for short.

The Bare-Knuckled Project Manager

The Right Person for the Job

Some management philosophies tell you that if you just follow these simple steps, you, too, can have perfect results. But it's never that simple.

Yes, there are always steps to follow and procedures to manage, but that leaves out the most essential part of the equation: the person. Anybody can walk up to the plate and swing a bat, but that doesn't mean everybody can become a major league superstar. It takes talent, temperament, skill, training, experience, attitude, and aptitude to be the best.

To implement Bare-Knuckled Project Management, you need a Bare-Knuckled Project Manager. Not everyone qualifies for the job.

Even if you do have what it takes, you still need the other elements: training, experience, and the right process. Throughout this book, we'll talk about the process. In this chapter, we'll talk about the person. Who is the bare-knuckled project manager? How do you find and develop that person?

Defining the Bare-Knuckled Project Manager

How is a Bare-Knuckled Project Manager different from a regular project manager?

The difference between a BKPM and a conventional project manager lies in the areas of attitude and skill. A conventional project manager knows the business of organizing and managing a project — but as we've seen, that's not enough to get the job done. A project manager needs to be a fighter as well as a planner. That's the core BKPM difference.

The word "fighter" may raise a few eyebrows or set off some alarms, but we can't afford to be politically correct when we talk about the reality of what a project manager faces. At the same time, we don't want to give you the wrong idea. A BKPM isn't a brawler, or somebody who looks for trouble. Instead, a BKPM is the one who settles a problem.

Thinking like a BKPM is similar to thinking like a martial artist, and there's no more famous martial artist than the legendary Bruce Lee. Best known for his movie roles, Lee also developed his own martial arts system and philosophy. Surprisingly, his philosophy has a lot to do with the real world of project management.

The Art of Fighting Without Fighting

Bruce Lee named his style *Jeet Kune Do*, but it was much more than a way of fighting. *Jeet Kune Do* is a philosophy of life, or as Bruce Lee called it, "the art of fighting without fighting."

Bruce Lee and Jeet Kune Do

Famed as an actor and considered by many the greatest martial artist of all time, Bruce Lee (李小龍) was a man for all seasons: actor, martial arts instructor, director, screenwriter, producer — and philosopher.

Born in 1940 in San Francisco's Chinatown, he moved to China and lived in Kowloon through adolescence, returning to the U.S. for higher education. Working first as a martial arts instructor, Lee became increasingly involved in film and television roles. Gaining American recognition for playing Kato in TV's *The Green Hornet*, Lee is credited for inspiring the modern American interest in martial arts.

After one season playing Kato, Lee, who had originally been trained in the martial art of Wing Chun, began to conclude that traditional martial arts were too rigid and formulistic. Starting in 1967, he began to develop the foundations of *Jeet Kune Do*, the "style of no style," a martial art that existed outside of parameters and limitations.

A highly intelligent and well-read man, Lee studied philosophy intensively, and developed an eclectic philosophy of his own that grew out of his martial arts approach, and included elements of Taoism, Buddhism, and Confucianism. He wrote poetry, practiced an intense discipline of physical training, and even developed his own approach to nutrition.

Lee died in 1973. The official cause of death was cerebral edema, possibly the result of an allergic reaction to medication.

Some of the principles of *Jeet Kune Do* have powerful applications when it comes to project management. Bruce Lee believed that traditional martial arts had become too rigid, and therefore unrealistic.

Much the same is true of modern project management, with its emphasis on getting a PMP® certificate that basically only shows that you've memorized a few books. There's a discipline and a process to project management, but it's easy to get lost in the formalities and lose track of the goal.

Combat, Bruce Lee says, is spontaneous. You can't predict it, but only react to it. That doesn't mean, however, that it isn't predictable or controllable.

In real life, project management follows the same model. "No battle plan survives first contact with the enemy" is an old military saying, and it's also true about every project. A project plan is useful, but it's a fatal mistake to take it too literally. Projects always contain surprises, and the BKPM has to react smoothly, even fluidly, and without hesitation — just like a fighter. The BKPM faces problems and solves them — simply and directly.

Core Competencies of the BKPM

That gives us the core competencies of a BKPM, shown in Figure 2-1. A BKPM is unafraid of conflict and confrontation; simple, direct, and effective; well disciplined; well trained and versatile; and moves forward consistently.

Figure 2-1. Core Competencies of the BKPM

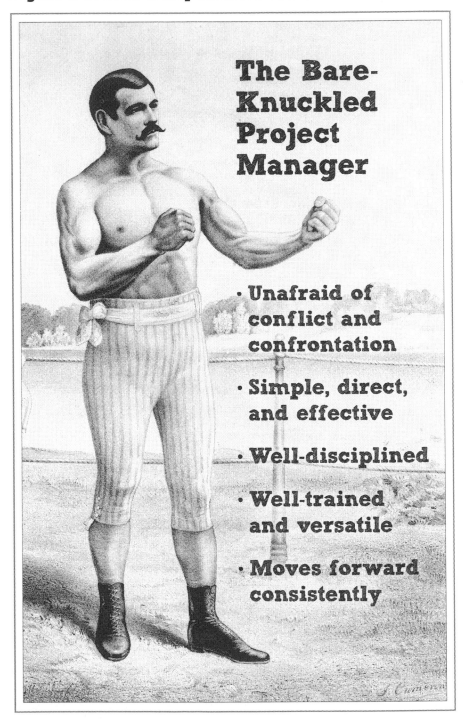

The Bare-Knuckled Project Manager

- Unafraid of conflict and confrontation
- Simple, direct, and effective
- Well-disciplined
- Well-trained and versatile
- Moves forward consistently

Unafraid of Conflict and Confrontation

No real fighter goes around picking fights, but real fighters aren't afraid to fight when the situation calls for it. Conflict happens every day, and the worst thing you can do is pretend that it isn't happening. If you're a kung-fu master or mixed martial artist, you don't go around looking for people to beat up — quite the contrary. Outside the ring, skilled fighters are often some of the nicest people you could ever hope to meet.

Inside the ring, however, they do what's necessary to get the job done.

Issues — and sometimes people — have to be confronted directly and firmly before they have a chance to get out of control. If you act early, it often takes less effort and involves less conflict than if you wait until the situation forces itself on you.

Of course, there are a lot of ways to handle a conflict or confrontation. Perhaps you can compromise or negotiate. But sometimes you have to be firm, direct, and final. Otherwise, you're not really being a project manager — much less a BKPM. (There's a lot more on how the BKPM handles conflict in Chapter Seven.)

It's important to note that this is most decidedly not standard human behavior. Most people will avoid conflict at almost any cost. They've learned that conflict results in bad things happening to someone, and that even winning a conflict probably means another fight down the road. BKPMs have the discipline to recognize conflicts early. They deal with the situation before there is even a clear winner and loser. In this way, problems get mutually resolved before they become outright battles.

When a battle does become necessary — and sometimes they're unavoidable — the BKPM will have already set up the conditions to be in their favor, much like a practiced martial artist would. Or as Sun Tzu puts it, "Victorious warriors win first and then go to war, while defeated warriors go to war first and then seek to win."

Simple, Direct, and Effective

If you watch a mixed martial arts (MMA) bare-knuckle fight, it doesn't look very much like a kung-fu movie. Instead of using elaborately choreographed fighting moves, real MMA fighters focus on the basics: simple, direct, and effective. Although they know the fancy moves, they also know that ninety percent of the time, it's the basics that carry the day. While a good martial artist knows all sorts of fighting techniques, in practice, a handful of straight, direct moves get used over and over again.

There are a seemingly unending number of fancy moves or special tools that a project manager might use: things like the Earned Value Method (EVM), the Program Evaluation and Review Technique (PERT), Monte Carlo simulations, critical path analysis, and network diagramming, along with lots of software to help you do it.

Every one of these tools has a time and a place where they're appropriate and effective. Most of the time, however, they're overkill. They add complexity and red tape and don't get the job done any faster or any better. In most cases, the simple and direct way is also the most effective. In other words, don't borrow trouble.

Although the BKPM has mastery (or at least a working familiarity) of the various tools of project management, the trick isn't to throw in the kitchen sink, but rather use the most important and valuable tools in a direct, simple, disciplined, and effective manner — a handful of straight, direct tools get about ninety percent of jobs done.

The BKPM's goal is never to do the project in the formal way — the goal is to do it the effective way. Results talk — bullshit walks. That's true no matter where the bullshit is coming from.

Disciplined

No matter how good you are at anything, you can always become better.

On the movie screen, Fred Astaire always looked like he was making up his dance moves spontaneously and effortlessly. In real life, the opposite was the case. Astaire was known as a demanding taskmaster, both of himself and others. His longtime partner Ginger Rogers said of him, "I thought I knew what concentrated work was before I met Fred, but he's the limit. Never satisfied until every detail is right, and he will not compromise."

Teamwork matters, too. As one critic observed, "Ginger Rogers did everything Fred Astaire did, except backwards and in high heels." A BKPM can't achieve greatness without helping teammates do the same thing.

You can't say you've mastered anything until it's reached the level of muscle memory — when your mind and body have learned it so well that it becomes virtually intuitive. That's called limbic learning, and we'll say more about it in Chapter Six.

Self-discipline, concentration, practice, and a commitment to excellence and perfection are the hallmark of any successful BKPM.

In managing our projects, discipline is essential. We have trained ourselves to follow practices so well that they become nearly unconscious ways of doing business. We create a plan, hold a kickoff meeting, designate a project website, schedule weekly calls, establish a weekly report, and expose the numbers. This allows us to prevent cost/resource surprises by showing the customer each and every week what the numbers are. We constantly focus on risk. Every report we do has a risk section.

Discipline in a few basic steps has taught us over and over again that about 80 percent of project risks are both predictable and preventable — as long as you have the systems in place to identify and deal with them early.

Over time, discipline and experience become art.

Well-Trained and Versatile

As we said, a project manager (BKPM or otherwise) ought to know the art. Command of the different tools makes a BKPM more versatile, and thus more effective.

Very little of that training, however, takes place in the classroom. Theory is no substitute for practical, on-the-job experience. A BKPM's training emphasizes practical learning.

Nobody, no matter how skilled, smart, or able, can become a BKPM overnight. BKPMs learn primarily by doing. They start as team members, develop technical skills, and experience the life cycle of projects. They get familiar with projects that fail as well as projects that succeed, and pay attention to the reasons for both success and failure.

BKPMs learn to adapt. They see the range of surprises and problems that crop up on projects, and they learn what to do and how to react to each category of challenge.

BKPMs learn to think in an uncomplicated manner. They avoid ornamentation or excessive formality. They focus on the goal and the best way to get there.

BKPMs learn to absorb what is useful and discard the rest. They see what works and what doesn't. If the tool isn't beneficial, it's discarded.

BKPMs are never dogmatic. They might have favorite ways of doing things, but they can put the favorite ways aside if that's what the situation calls for. Organizations are different. Projects are different. One size never fits all.

How do you achieve that? Discipline. The disciplined use of tools, practice, perseverance, time-on-task, and experience eventually gives way to art. There's no shortcut.

Moves Forward Consistently

Bruce Lee explained his philosophy this way: "My movements are simple, direct, and non-classical. The extraordinary part of it lies in its simplicity. I always believe the easy way is the right way. *Jeet Kune Do* is simply the direct expression of one's feelings with the minimum of movement and energy."

The best defense, as we know, is a good offense. You must approach the target to engage with it. Sometimes you speed up; sometimes you slow down. Sometimes you expand; sometimes you contract — but you always move forward.

The commitment to forward movement is also a discipline. Even if the goal isn't crystal clear (which is most of the time), we can still make progress if we're moving in the right general direction. Incremental improvement through continual progress eventually reaches the desired goal.

Now, let's see how the BKPM fits into the rest of the project and the process.

The Three-Sided Table

Running the Table

O F ALL of the practices presented in this book, the concept of managing a project as if the BKPM is sitting at a three-sided table is one of the most fundamental.   Almost everything else is designed to maintain this relationship between project owners and fulfillment teams.

Of course, no project manager, not even the most highly skilled, can do it alone. Executive leadership sets the tone and provides the support; project sponsors establish the goals; the solutions team partners to do the work; and the project manager runs the plan and process. Establishing clear goals, roles, and expectations for the different project players is a necessary precondition for the BKPM.

In traditional project management, the PM / customer / team relationship can be described as a two-sided table: the project manager and team on one side, and the customer or client on the other, as shown in Figure 3-1.

At first glance, this makes perfect sense. The project manager, after all, leads the team, and is accountable for delivering results to the customer. That makes the project manager the advocate and architect of the team's solution. When the team succeeds, the project manager succeeds. When the team fails, the project manager fails.

The customer, on the other hand, is independent. The job of the customer is to articulate what he or she wants, and ultimately to pay for it. That means the customer's role is to put pressure on the project manager and team to deliver the right solution on the right timetable at the right price.

But in the BKPM approach, that's absolutely wrong.

Figure 3-1. Traditional Project Management. In the traditional project management situation, the customer/client sits on one side of the table, and the project manager and team sit on the other side.

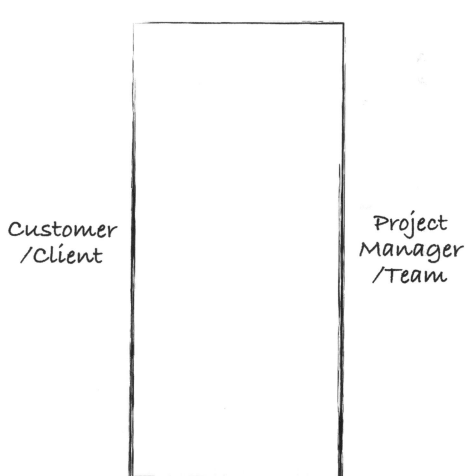

From Two-Sided to Three-Sided

The BKPM approach makes some changes to conventional project management. One of these is to change how we view the relationship of the BKPM to the team and to the customer or sponsor. We call it the *Three-Sided Table*, and it's a powerful tool to reframe the role of project manager in the process of getting the work done.

The Three-Sided Table View

Let's talk first about how the three-sided table works, and then we'll talk about its benefits to you and the project. In the three-sided table approach, every project has three "seats" that must be filled:

- The **customer or executive sponsor** owns the *outcome*, not the *process*. This is absolutely critical. If the executive sponsor cannot clearly articulate the desired project outcome in terms of business impact, then there is little chance that it will be reached.

- The **project manager** owns the *process*, not the *outcome*. Again, this is critical. This position of purity is exactly what enables consistent project success.

- The **partners and team** align with the *direction* of the project manager to achieve the *technical objectives* of the project. They are the primary consumers of time and budget and, in the end, render products or services.

Figure 3-2. Three-Sided Table. In the three-sided table approach, the project manager is independent of both the client/customer and the partners/implementation team.

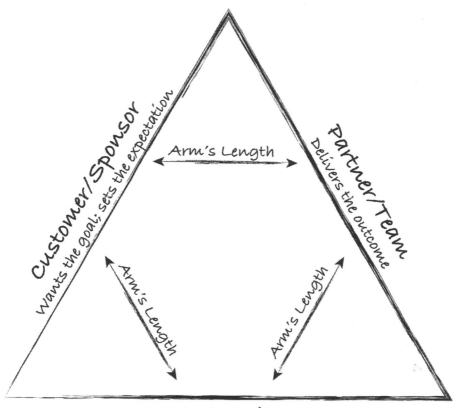

Bare-Knuckled Project Manager
Architect and manager of the plan and process

Project managers traditionally manage the "triple constraint" (Chapter Four): on time, on budget, and to spec. But that's not how the executive sponsor should look at it.

The value of a project *to you* is how it impacts your business. If a job's not worth doing in the first place, it hardly matters if it's on time and on budget; if the project is valuable enough to your business objectives, over budget or behind schedule may not be that important.

Some executive sponsors link the project outcome to the project manager and team, giving them a handy way to spread the blame when things go wrong, but that turns a project into a death spiral. You can't afford to do that. Here's why.

As an executive, you have a different perspective than that of the project manager and fulfillment team. They may not be aware of how all the business's moving parts fit together — and it has to be that way. That's why you must *never make the project manager or fulfillment team responsible for a single project's outcome.*

When you violate this rule, you end up with a two-sided table, with the PM and team on one side and the customer/ executive sponsor on the other. Because you have a perspective and critical knowledge that the PM/team does not, the PM/team focuses on achieving whatever outcome you told them in the most direct way possible.

In the famous case of the Ford Pinto, engineers were tasked to build a small car that weighed no more than 2,000 pounds and cost no more than $2,000 in 1968 dollars (about $13,000 in 2012). They achieved every one of their technical specifications — but the infamous gas tank problem nearly sank the company because they couldn't afford the extra $11 per car to make it safer.

Ultimately, that's not a technical failure, but a leadership failure. Technical teams are supposed to do what they're told. If they're told the wrong thing, it's not their fault that they do it. In the two-sided table, the PM and team have one goal: achieve whatever outcome you gave them in the most direct way possible, *regardless of the real effect on your business.*

Life is full of situations that fit the model, "The operation was a success but the patient died."

Because you as an executive sponsor can't — and shouldn't — spend your day micromanaging the project manager and team, you need someone who can keep both sides (you and the implementation team) working to achieve the right kind of success.

By using the three-sided table approach, the organization, the project team, and the customer realize important benefits, including:

- The BKPM finds out the truth and shares it. There are no secrets with the BKPM; he or she is the honest broker to both sides.

- The BKPM holds everyone's feet to the fire. This means not only being accountable, but constantly moving the ball forward.

- The BKPM determines if risk is within acceptable boundaries.

- The BKPM challenges the proposed technical solutions and approaches.

- The BKPM has profit and loss (P&L) accountability for the project.

- The BKPM keeps unnecessary escalations away from senior executives — and lets them sleep at night.

As we've seen, in conventional project management models the project manager and the team are considered to be on the same side — a two-sided table. But in the BKPM method, we extract the project manager from the team, and thereby move the BKPM away from a defensive position in the relationship.

In other words, the BKPM doesn't represent the solutions team any more than he or she represents the sponsor. That frees the BKPM to focus on the plan and the process of project execution in line with overall business objectives.

The Three-Sided Table View

In the three-sided table, every project has three "seats" that must be filled.

Customer/Sponsor/Outcome Owner

The customer or sponsor is the person or group in an organization that wants the specific outcome of a project. That person or group can be inside or outside the performing organization.

Generally, we use "sponsor" if that person or group is internal, and "customer" if external. Examples of sponsors can be the boss, the president, the COO, or a department head. Customers are the clients who are paying to have the job done.

A project can have a sponsor as well as a customer, if there's an internal leader who serves as the inside customer voice.

That's why the customer/sponsor — and only the customer/sponsor — can be the outcome owner. It's your responsibility, your vision, and your ability to understand your customers and stakeholders.

Partner/Team/Implementer

The partner or team consists of the people who are responsible for delivering the specific outcome desired by the sponsor or the customer. Partners can be internal (staff) or external (subcontractors), or both.

Technical teams, not the customer/sponsor, are the experts in the "how" of the project, but not the experts in "why." Sometimes they'll tell you why a particular job can't be done, or why another method is preferable.

Whether they're right or not depends on what the business goal actually is.

If you tell people that their job is to get it done cheap, and putting the gas tank over a bolt (as in the Pinto) is the best way to do it cheaply, then that's what the technical team will do. That's their job.

Of course, good technical teams will point out the consequences of that choice (as the Ford engineers did), but it's not up to them to force the change.

BKPM/Process Owner

The BKPM is the arm's length architect of the plan and process, and sits between the sponsor/customer and the partner/team. The BKPM owns the process. In meetings, we say, "He who owns the agenda, controls the meeting." For the BKPM, "he who owns the process, controls the progress."

In our experience, BKPMs perform better when they are independent from the development team as well as from the customer/sponsor, hence the three-sided table. That arms-length relationship is essential for the BKPM to perform his or her role.

In the case of the Pinto, the technical team had a lot of trouble being listened to by management. The same thing was true on another failed project, the Space Shuttle Challenger. In both cases, there was a failure of process because there was nobody empowered to broker the right agreement between executive management and the team. (The same problem occurred on Apollo until a BKPM — Gene Krantz — stepped in, as described in Chapter 8.)

If the project manager is simply part of the team, then the project manager will take on the team's perspective, and that leaves executive management out of the loop. You don't want that.

GREAT and the BKPM

The GREAT model of team building identifies the critical elements needed for success. A BKPM makes sure each of these is clear, understood, and accepted by everyone involved with the project. "GREAT" stands for:

Goals

Roles

Expectations

Attitude and Aptitude

Time

Let's look at these one by one.

Goals

Goals exist at many levels on the same project. There is an overall project goal, the desired outcome, but to achieve it, other participants have to accomplish their own subordinate goals.

For the customer, the most essential goal is a successful outcome.

For the BKPM, the goal is a great process that results in a satisfied customer. For the team, the goal is to provide a technical solution that falls within the project constraints.

Roles

In the three-sided table, we assign specific roles to the different players in the process. Each performs a necessary function; each checks and balances the others.

We've established that the BKPM owns the process. This management includes being an honest broker between the parties — forcing the customer to own the outcome and driving the team to achieve an appropriate technical solution.

For the customer, the essential role is to define clearly and usefully what the desired outcome looks like. The outcome may have nothing to do directly with the technical solution — the people who need IT solutions often aren't part of IT themselves, nor should they be.

The team must find a technical solution that achieves the desired outcome — if the new IT system doesn't solve the customer need, it doesn't matter how quickly, cheaply, or elegantly it was done.

Expectations

Each role has expectations for what the other roles will be doing, and the standard to which they will do it. One of the ongoing responsibilities of the BKPM is to make sure those expectations are appropriate and honored.

The customer expects that the team will provide a workable solution; the team expects that the customer will be able to say what he or she wants.

The BKPM, being experienced in the ways of organizations, expects that both customer and team will fail to do this as well as necessary, and will step in to make sure it's done right before moving any farther with the project.

The other two sides may not expect this, but they will be grateful in the long run when it is done.

Attitude and Aptitude

Political problems, personality issues, or simple disgruntlement complicate most projects enormously. All too often, the prevailing management response is to ignore the problem and hope it goes away on its own. This is often a contributing cause to project failure.

It's human nature to have some degree of on-the-job friction. You can make it better, but you can't make it go away. As a BKPM, your first need is to understand where people are. You don't have to approve it or agree with it, but you will inevitably have to work with it.

Equally, members of the team may not possess all the skills and abilities necessary to accomplish a particular solution. It's often possible to overcome these limitations, but only if you know what they are in advance. As a BKPM, learn what people can and cannot do so you can define your strong spots and your weak spots — and do something about it.

Time

Whether or not the project is deadline driven, it always has a tempo. As we've learned, the BKPM's motto is "always move forward," but that's not a project's natural tendency.

Projects, like every other thing in nature, are subject to inertia. When at rest, they tend to stay at rest. The only way a project moves forward is through the application of energy, and that's an essential part of the BKPM's function.

What's the next milestone? How can we get there? How can we keep our forward momentum from stalling out?

Defining Roles and Responsibilities

As we've seen, these three roles — BKPM, customer, team — interact in a specific manner, each with defined roles, responsibilities, goals, as shown in Figure 3-3.

Figure 3-3. Roles and Accountability. Each part of the three-sided table has specific roles and areas of accountability.

Role	Owns the...	Relationship to Project Manager/ BKPM	Relationship to Customer/ Sponsor	Relationship to Partner/ Team/ Implementer
Project Manager	Process		Forces clarity and owner-ship, delivers results	Validates technical solution, enforces milestones
Customer/ Sponsor	Outcome	Provides clarity and ownership, defines schedule and budget		Validates deliverables, controls scope
Partner/ Team/ Imple-menter	Technical Objectives	Makes and adheres to promises, develops solution	Adjusts scope, provides deliverables	

In summary:

- The **customer or executive sponsor** owns the *outcome,* not the *process.*
- The **project manager** owns the *process,* not the *outcome.*
- The **partners and team** align with the *direction* of the project manager to achieve the *technical objectives* of the project.

These three separate roles and how they interact is critical to the BKPM method.

BKPM Issues

In the three-sided table, the BKPM is the honest broker, who does not represent a particular interest. The BKPM *owns only the plan and the process*, but *not* the outcome and *not* the technical solution! The BKPM serves as the honest broker, negotiator, and arbitrator who makes the process work.

Strangely, if the BKPM becomes too emotionally invested in the outcome, rather than the process, it hurts the three-sided table, and ultimately the project itself. The BKPM becomes co-opted by the customer's side, and no longer has the ability to balance outcome objectives with technical reality.

The other direction is equally problematic. If the BKPM becomes too deeply allied with the implementation team, the need to deliver a technical solution can override the need for that solution to achieve the customer's desired outcome. We've all seen projects where the implementation team points proudly to a solution ("It's done!") and yet the customer's fundamental needs have not really been met.

While the BKPM's investment in one side or the other doesn't itself cause the project to fail, it significantly increases the risk. As soon as the BKPM stops being seen as an honest broker, communication begins to break down, and the needs and goals of the other two sides of the table naturally begin to drift apart.

While investing in the outcome doesn't itself cause the project to fail, but it does increase the risk. We refer to this as *co-opt risk*.

That's not to argue that emotional involvement on the part of the BKPM is wrong — quite the contrary. Emotional investment can be very positive, as long as it's invested in the right direction. For the BKPM, that means emotional investment in having the best, most foolproof process; anticipating and managing all known risks; and solving the inevitable problems that crop up on even the best-run project are all wonderful goals.

Sponsor/Customer Issues

The sponsor or customer is responsible for articulating the desired outcome in sufficient detail to allow the solution team to craft a solution within the boundaries of the Triple Constraints — time, cost, and performance criteria.

By definition, the customer/sponsor *owns the outcome* of the project. The customer naturally has the clearest insight and understanding of the potential impacts of success or failure. The customer/sponsor also has the best understanding of the level of scope change that the organization can bear in order to realize the benefits of the project. Only the outcome owner can make certain project decisions related to the organization as a whole.

Many times, the outcome owner cannot or does not explain all of the impact, the politics, and the relationship of the project to the overall organizational strategy or tactical deployment. For that reason, other project participants might think that the outcome owner is making terrible decisions, but they have no way of knowing all customer actions or understanding of the ultimate outcome of the project.

Partner/Team Issues

The partner or implementation team is responsible for *crafting the solution* to reach the outcome desired by the customer or sponsor, within the boundaries of the Triple Constraint: how can we achieve the outcome within an acceptable time frame and at an acceptable cost?

It's the solution team, not the BKPM, who has this responsibility. It's the job of the BKPM to force the solution team to define what can be done, how long it will take, and how much it will cost.

What if the outcome can't be achieved within the boundaries of time and cost? That's certainly a problem, but if that's the reality, it's always better to know it up front, before the project begins. The same thing is true if the solution is risky — it's something we haven't done before, or we're taking on a challenge at the very edge of our capabilities.

Sometimes it's necessary to negotiate between the customer and the implementation team, and that's another reason it's so critical to have the BKPM in a position to serve as the honest broker.

The BKPM as Honest Broker

Serving as honest broker, negotiator, and arbitrator is an essential part of the job of the BKPM. As an independent part of the three-sided table, the BKPM remains at arm's length from the other two sides to ensure that everyone involved does his or her job. Risk evaluation, assessment, and mitigation are an active part of this process.

The BKPM can't afford to take ownership of matching customer requirements to team deliverables. If the customer or sponsor hasn't yet made it clear what the desired outcome is, the BKPM can't permit the partner/team to end up with responsibility for managing a muddle.

Similarly, the BKPM has to make sure that the potential solution is properly validated. Is the process reasonable? Is the focus on achieving the outcome? Are the assumptions of the implementation team appropriate and realistic?

In this process, the BKPM works with both of the other sides of the three-sided table. There is often some back-and-forth before all parties get on the same page with a solution that works. Sometimes one side or another has to give a little bit. Sometimes, the goals and project parameters have to be revised.

But all of this *must* take place before the work of the project begins.

Forcing the Customer

The BKPM's job in this relationship is to *force* the sponsor/customer, who is usually senior to the BKPM in the organization, or is a client of the BKPM's own organization, to *own* the clear articulation of the desired outcome.

And yes, *forcing* is often the right word. Just because a sponsor or customer wants something, it doesn't mean that he or she truly understands it well enough to articulate it.

Sometimes, the sponsor or customer resists being clear about the desired outcome as a way to avoid responsibility if things go wrong. If the project manager accepts this, and doesn't force a clear and definitive articulation, the project is in deep trouble — and usually, the project manager ends up being blamed. The BKPM *never* allows this to happen. If the sponsor or customer won't go on the record about the goal, the project stops right there.

Of course, that's never the goal anyone wants. Instead, the BKPM leads a process of *forced clarification*.

It takes courage — and usually risk — for a BKPM to take this responsibility, but think of the alternative. If you don't know where you're going in the first place, it's not realistic to expect to find a way to get there.

The customer or sponsor must own the outcome. That's their fundamental role. Most of the time, a sponsor likes the idea of being crystal clear, and will agree to that as a requirement process requirement. This is key for the BKPM. Sponsors do not always understand how difficult it can be to achieve clarity, but because they have already committed to it, they are forced to be clear in order for the project to proceed. In other words, force is applied by *agreement*, not by *confrontation*.

The most important step in forced clarification is the focus on *why*. A project is not an end in itself, but rather a means to an end. The more you can clarify the desired end state (the "why" of the project), the easier it becomes to define the "what" (objectives) and "how" (methodology). To do that, the BKPM asks probing questions, some of which are shown in Figure 3-4.

Figure 3-4. Forced Clarification. Asking probing questions is the key to forced clarification of project objectives. In particular, "why" is often the most overlooked question in project management.

- Why are we doing this?
- What's the gap between the current situation and the goal we want to reach?
- How will things be different if we succeed with this project? How will things be different if we fail or if we don't do it at all?
- What are the dangers of success? What are the benefits of failure?
- What are we assuming about the world around us when we conceive of this project?
- How much is it worth to us to solve the issue at hand?

The Power of Why

Project objectives lay out the "what" of a project: a spelled-out goal, defined requirements, deliverables, and other quantifiable measurements that correspond to project success.

Project managers and project teams develop the "how" of a project during planning: timelines, budgets, work assignments, and status reporting. Most projects are doing well just to get to the "what" and "how," rather than blindly heading off into the wilderness hoping to stumble upon success.

Very few projects ever get to "why." Why do we need a new IT system? Why do we need to expand our staff? Why are we performing these steps in paying an invoice?

Supplement your "why" questions with "what ifs." What if we kept our existing system? What if we reduced our staff? What if we missed some of the steps in paying an invoice?

If you don't know what the problem is, or what the solution does (and doesn't) do, all the project management in the world won't improve your situation.

- How are the problems that this project is supposed to solve being handled right now?

- How does this project fit in with the other priorities and goals of the program?

- How good does the solution have to be to solve the problem adequately?

- What would a perfect solution look like?

- Who has a stake in the outcome of the project? What does the outcome look like for each stakeholder?

- Do we really understand the problem or the solution?

In one case, we had a client engaged in a lean manufacturing effort to find ways to reduce operating costs. One step in the quality control process involved X-raying the welds in a containment vessel, finding and repairing any microscopic defects in the weld, and after that pressure testing the vessel to make sure it would hold.

The performance record of the tests revealed that whether or not the microscopic defects were repaired, the vessels *always and without exception* passed the pressure test. Given that the X-raying and repair step took time and cost money, it appeared as if that step could be skipped with no degradation of quality whatsoever.

One staff engineer, however, took the time to ask *why*. If there was never a problem with vessels failing the pressure test, why were the X-rays added in the first place? Upon investigation, the secret was revealed: the vessels *used* to fail pressure testing quite regularly, not because of microscopic defects in the welds, but because of grosser errors. When the welding contractor received the X-rays showing visible defects, it inspired greater quality assurance efforts on the part of the contractor, and greater effort on the part of the welders themselves to do an outstanding job.

In other words, the X-rays were very important indeed — but their effect on quality was psychological rather than literal. Worse, subsequent engineers who didn't understand the underlying "why" had gone to more expensive and thorough X-raying of the welds, adding cost without adding value! Asking *why* allowed the company to save money without creating a new defect problem in the process.

Forcing the Team

Additionally, the implementation team defines the lack of clarity. The implementation team is used as a lever to judge the level of clarity needed in order to be successful. In order to scope a project successfully, the implementation team must create deliverables that it can achieve and it must properly define and limit those deliverables.

Furthermore, the outcome owner must agree to the deliverables and to the limits put upon them. Failure to reach agreement keeps the project from progressing. The BKPM facilitates this process until both opposing seats of the table are satisfied.

The BKPM participates in this process by exposing risks that must be addressed by both other parties. The BKPM also participates by measuring and portraying the level of risk being assumed by the project caused by any less-than-clear deliverables or specifications and develops acceptable mitigation plans to deal with them if/when they are encountered.

Here's another advantage of keeping the BKPM separate from this process. First, if the solution team has to go back to tell the customer that he or she can't have the outcome within the cost and time constraints, there's usually pushback. If the BKPM is part of the process, the BKPM can't be an honest broker. But an honest broker is exactly what's necessary when this happens.

First, the BKPM has to review the solution. Is the team working hard enough or smart enough? If not, the BKPM has to force them to find a better way.

Second, the BKPM has to make sure that any technical solution is honest: that it's a reasonable approach that doesn't require ridiculously compressed timelines, cost overruns or hidden costs, or — worst of all — burned-out teams.

Third, once the BKPM is satisfied that the solution team has done the best job possible, the BKPM has to take the solution to the customer. If there's a conflict (cost, time, performance, or risk isn't within boundaries), it becomes the BKPM's responsibility as honest broker to negotiate and arbitrate the solution.

Yes, sometimes that means the project doesn't go forward. But it's cheaper to deal with that up front rather than wait for an expensive failure before everyone realizes that it was doomed from the start.

Similar to the discussion above about the word "force," because the BKPM owns the process, we can insert gates in the plan that make it impossible to proceed without a sufficient level of clarity in the deliverables being committed to by the solution team. This gate is usually all of the force that is needed to compel the solution team to provide the level of detail necessary and level of commitment necessary to the project deliverables. Deliverables are not the same as outcome. Often time, deliverables can change and still satisfy the outcome owners. There is usually more than one way to skin that cat.

The BKPM and the Process

Of course, that's not nearly all the BKPM does. The BKPM must manage the process, and that includes many other issues.

- Preparing (or at least validating) the overall plan.
- Making sure that customers and team members know about changes and issues as they arise.
- Establishing milestones to ensure that the project consistently moves forward.
- Keeping the focus on achieving the outcome, rather than getting buried in the technical details.
- Choosing the best way forward when presented with alternative approaches.

Not everybody can do this job. As we've learned, there are a number of characteristics of the BKPM — but we've left off one. The BKPM must have the credibility with both the sponsor and the team to force the process and ensure that everyone takes ownership.

In the actual process of managing the project, the BKPM takes the lead, making sure that everyone sticks to what they've agreed to. When problems arise, the BKPM continues to manage the three-sided table, forcing sponsors and team members alike to face the challenges of the project head on and to make whatever course corrections are needed. The key to this process is exposing the issues and making sure that it is discussed and resolved.

And, as we've already learned, the BKPM *moves forward consistently*.

Payoffs from the Three-Sided Table

When the project manager is considered part of the team itself, rather than an independent part of the three-sided table approach, the project manager is part of management when deciding about the goals and objectives, and part of the team when advocating a technical solution. That creates a tendency for the project manager to become an *advocate*, not an *analyst*, for the two sides. This isn't optimal.

There's often a conflict between what the customer wants and the team says they can deliver, and someone has to decide. If it's the customer, the team can be forced into an impossible situation. If it's the team, the customer may be paying a lot more than needed to solve the problem. You need an honest broker, someone who stands outside the conflict, to make it happen. That's the BKPM.

Managers aren't always the subject matter experts about the type of work being done in the project. Many people who need IT solutions aren't IT professionals, for example. If you push the team into an impossible project, nobody's going to win.

What you want is the *truth*. (And you *can* handle the truth.)

Teams don't always understand the wider context. Some requirements on a project may be flexible, but others are absolute, and which is which depends on the circumstances. Those circumstances aren't always obvious to outsiders. Just because you tell the team the requirement is absolute doesn't mean it really is, or that they believe you. What they need, as much as you, is the truth, whatever it might be.

The BKPM holds everyone's feet to the fire. The BKPM challenges the assumptions and ideas that the customer or sponsor puts forward. Is the objective clear and specific enough to allow the team to work effectively? Are the triple constraints of time, cost, and essential performance reasonable? Is risk within bounds?

The BKPM challenges the proposed technical solutions and approaches that the team comes up with. Are they reasonable approaches to achieving the project within the triple constraint? What's the level of risk?

As process owner, the BKPM is the escalation point for most project issues, freeing the senior executives on the customer side from dealing with any but the most serious and far-reaching issues. The BKPM pulls in executives only when necessary — letting them sleep at night.

Finally, the BKPM is the person who needs to *stop* the project and hold the right people accountable if the goals and the solution can't be brought together.

Because the BKPM owns the *process*, the BKPM has P&L accountability for the project's success or failure. The BKPM won't let the project go forward until there's a reasonable prospect of success. That's in *everybody's* best interest.

No Bullshit
Project
Management

A Poor Workman Blames His Tools

A CLIENT once asked us to recommend some project management software, and said that he'd tried Microsoft Project® and he really didn't like it very much. He was wondering if Oracle Primavera® (an enterprise-level system) would be more appropriate.

We asked about the kinds of project the client did. They were relatively small: usually under $50,000, involving teams of three to five people, and taking six to nine weeks.

Our immediate assumption was that project management software might not be necessary at all, but we asked one final question: what exactly was it that he didn't like about Microsoft Project®.

"It keeps trying to do something called a Gantt chart," he said, "but it won't tell me what a Gantt chart is!"

There are any number of good books on the techniques and tools of classical project management, and it's not our intention to repeat them here. If you need to know what a Gantt chart is (it's a bar graph of the project activities on a timeline), you can find that information many other places.

What's more, it's not always important. While we often use Gantt charts ourselves, we don't make a fetish out of them. Sometimes a list of critical milestones and interim dates is all you really need.

With all the modern emphasis on getting PMP® certified, using cutting-edge project management software, and following a detailed process, something gets lost. We fail to see the forest for the trees; we mistake lots of paperwork for lots of real work.

The dirty little secret of project management is that it costs time and money to do it right. If you're running a $10 million project, even $1 million might not be too much to spend on project management if you can guarantee you'll be on time and on budget. It all depends on the complexity of the moving parts that need to be coordinated. But if you're running a $10,000 project, you'll be long since done with the work before you could get halfway through a formal plan. One size most definitely doesn't fit all.

The truth is that the $10,000 project can get along just fine without much in the way of a formal plan. The $10 million project, on the other hand, really needs a whole lot more in the way of control and oversight. One of the first jobs of the BKPM is to decide when it comes to project management, how much you really think you need.

A lot of formal project management, in our opinion, is overkill. You can spend more time making fancy-looking reports and charts than you spend actually managing the project. That doesn't provide a benefit for anybody — customer, team, or BKPM.

The basic rule is simple: Don't drive carpet tacks with a sledgehammer.

In this chapter, we'll explore how the bare-knuckled approach differs from traditional PMI/PMBOK® project management. Which tools of project management do we use, which do we modify, and which do we ignore?

Let's take a look.

Establish Goals and Objectives (Project Initiation)

We've established that the customer must own the outcome, and we've also established that this is a lot easier said than done. Customers don't always understand their own needs, aren't always able to articulate them, and sometimes have a motivation to keep them from the prying eyes of team members. The BKPM's role, as we've learned, is to *force* the process as part of getting everyone on the same page.

What is a project? PMI defines it as "temporary and unique," and so it is. But more importantly, a project is a *means to an end*. We launch a project because we have some kind of issue: a problem, an opportunity, or a change. To resolve the issue, we first have to define it. In other words, before we ask what's the *project*, we need to ask what's the *problem*.

Let's say that we're delaying sending out invoices to customers because our process takes too long. That's a *problem*, but that doesn't tell us immediately what the *project* should be. Is it an IT solution? Is it a management problem? Does the problem lie in accounts receivable, or is it somewhere else? Our answers to these questions help turn the *problem* into a *project*.

Let's assume we learn that yes, the problem is in accounts receivable and, further, that it lies within the IT realm. Now we have to quantify it. How fast are we processing invoices now, and how fast do we *want* or *need* to process them in the future? As we answer those questions, we begin to define the *outcome* we want.

In developing the *technical solution*, we need both the team and the BKPM involved. While some customers are highly knowledgeable about IT, others are not. They cannot necessarily tell from a proposed technical solution whether it's going to achieve the outcome. Again, the BKPM, serving as honest broker, works with both sides to make sure (a) the technical solution is valid and can be done within cost and time parameters, and (b) that the technical solution will in fact achieve the outcome.

In developing the *process*, the BKPM, as process owner, takes the lead. That's the project management piece. It involves planning, risk management, communication, and project leadership.

Don't ever assume that people will automatically or naturally end up on the same page. This assumption has sunk any number of projects. The BKPM's role is to *force* the process, and to ensure that the final product is written down and agreed to by the participants. (In formal project management speak, we call the process "initiating the project" and the written statement of what we're going to do is the "project charter.")

Setting the objective and validating the technical approach within the triple constraints is the first step in any project. Mess that up, and *nothing* else you do will be enough to compensate. That's the essence of strategic project management. It's hard work, it's challenging, and it all too often gets political.

When the Answer is Unknown

Even if every stakeholder is positive, hard working, insightful, intelligent, and able to put all politics aside (as unlikely as that sounds), it may not be enough to establish a meaningful objective. Sometimes, there's just too much that isn't known. We have an idea of the general direction; we may even have an idea what the eventual outcome needs to be; but we just don't know enough about the work or the challenges or the details of the vision to come up with a concrete objective.

What now?

As any research scientist will tell you, just because you don't know what you're looking for or how to go about finding it, it doesn't mean you can't move forward. The experimental method is *iterative*. We try again and again.

Thomas Edison wrote about the development of the light bulb, "During all those years of experimentation and research, I never once made a discovery. All my work was deductive, and the results I achieved were those of invention, pure and simple. I would construct a theory and work on its lines until I found it was untenable. Then it would be discarded at once and another theory evolved. This was the only possible way for me to work out the problem. ... I speak without exaggeration when I say that I have constructed 3,000 different theories in connection with the electric light, each one of them reasonable and apparently likely to be true. Yet only in two cases did my experiments prove the truth of my theory."

One of the big topics in contemporary project is known as "agile development," in which requirements for engineering and technology development projects are determined iteratively. Regular project management has the challenge that sometimes customers can't develop requirements up front; they need prototypes. By building something, examining it, learning lessons, and trying again, projects that can't be done in a single cycle can be achieved in multiple cycles.

The downside, of course, is that these kinds of projects often take longer and cost more money, so if you really do know your requirements in advance, everyone's better off. But sometimes that just isn't possible. The choice is between spending the necessary time and money or not doing the project at all.

If you have to follow this course, patience is necessary. As Edison added, "Many of life's failures are people who did not realize how close they were to success when they gave up."

Good, Fast, or Cheap? (Triple Constraints)

When you do have validated requirements and are ready to get to work, you have additional challenges. For example, everybody in management sooner or later hears the old joke, "Did you want it good, fast, or cheap? Pick two." Of course, our immediate reaction is that we'd prefer to pick all three, but it's inarguable that there's often tension among the competing demands of a project and the constraints under which it operates.

The classic "triple constraint" model focuses on the three elements that are common to virtually every project: the cost constraint (budget and resource), the time constraint (schedule and deadline), and the performance criteria (the minimum necessary to achieve success). There are, of course, many other constraints that may apply, such as the level of risk, the need for quality, and the presence of regulations and standards.

Figure 4-1 illustrates the Triple Constraints model. While issues of risk and quality are constraining, their application to each specific project varies. Time, cost, and scope, however, are universal.

Figure 4-1. Triple Constraints. The universal issues of time, cost, and scope apply to every project.

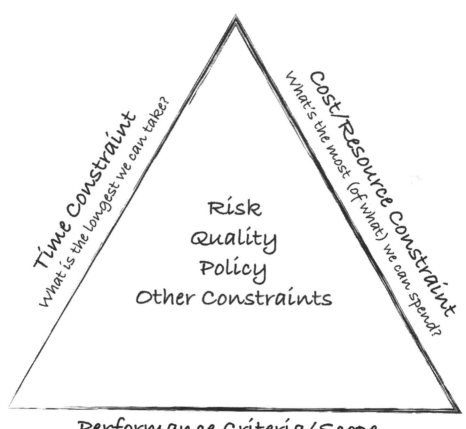

Hierarchy of Constraints

The idea that success in one constraint can only be achieved at the cost of another constraint ("pick two") is misleading and wrong. You *can* have all three — at least some of the time. Some constraints are absolute — violate them and bad things happen. Others, though, may have flexibility.

The constraints are normally ranked in a hierarchy based on the goals of the project — the *why* sets the priorities.

- The **driver** is the constraint central to the definition of success. If you fail to meet the driver, you fail to achieve the outcome.

- The **weak constraint** is the most flexible of the three, but is not always or necessarily the least important.

- The **middle constraint,** as the name suggests, falls in between the two.

Sometimes, there's flexibility in the timing. We'd prefer a shorter schedule to a longer one, but there is no hard-and-fast deadline. Sometimes, there's flexibility in the budget. We'd prefer to spend less, but if necessary we'll spend more. And finally, sometimes there's flexibility in the performance requirements — some requirements may even be optional.

In planning your project, you *must* plan to achieve the project driver at all costs. The legitimate flexibility in the other constraints is a vital tool in that process.

For a sense of the Triple Constraints in action, think about the Apollo program.

Apollo and the Triple Constraints

In his famous 1961 speech, President John F. Kennedy established the Apollo program with the following Triple Constraints.

- **Time:** "Before this decade is out"
- **Performance:** "Landing a man on the Moon and returning him safely to the Earth"
- **Cost:** Unspecified — to be determined by Congress

What's the hierarchy? Most people would say the driver is *performance*, getting there and back safely.

But think about *why* are we doing the project. The motivation for the Apollo program was the space race with the Soviet Union. Coming in second won't do. That made *time* (not "the end of the decade," but rather "before the Soviets") the driver. Performance was the *middle constraint*, and cost was *weak*. That seems pretty cold, but it's realistic. A single mission failure wouldn't kill the program.

In managing this project, solve problems first by spending money and second by taking more risk — but you can't compromise the schedule.

But in the Space Shuttle program, which wasn't a race, cost was the driver, followed by performance, with time bringing up the rear. As your driver changes, so does the right decision.

Designing a Process (Planning)

Based on the understanding of the desired *outcome*, the nature of the *technical solution*, and the environment of constraints, the role of the BKPM is to establish the right *process*. That's the process of project planning.

The *process* consists of a technical approach (there may be several to choose from), a timeline of the work necessary to get there, and a resource budget (which includes money, of course, but also every other needed resource that's in limited supply).

The *goal* is a clear, concise statement of what you want the end state to look like. Notice that's not always identical to the project *objectives*, which is what the team is supposed to deliver. As we've established, if you procure a new IT system, it's not because you want a new IT system as such. You want the new IT system to solve a problem, make an improvement, or take advantage of an opportunity. That's the *goal*. It's when you start translating a goal into objectives that you start running into trouble. It's not as easy as it looks.

Sometimes the IT team will list a series of objectives that will improve the IT system as such, but won't affect how well it achieves the goal. Or management will propose an objective that doesn't actually achieve the goal, usually out of a misunderstanding or the need to sound smart. Once that happens, your project once again is compromised. That's why an independent BKPM, loyal only to the process, is so critical to your success.

Finding the Most Efficient Path

Since both *objectives* and *solutions* are on the table, the customer and the team are brought together, facilitated by the BKPM, to find the most efficient way to achieve the outcome. The customer is confronted when the goal isn't realistic or achievable within the constraints, and the team is confronted with the need to offer a credible, real solution.

The BKPM facilitates the process, but owns neither the goal nor the solution, as we've seen. From the BKPM's perspective, the project becomes an entrepreneurial endeavor. The BKPM is cast as an "interim owner," or as an "outcome advocate." That frees the BKPM to adapt as the situation may require, always steering toward the goal no matter what winds or waves buffet the ship.

The Project as Entrepreneurial Enterprise

A project, temporary and unique as it is, disrupts the organization around it. Temporary supervisor/subordinate relationships add complexity to the chain of command. Some people are no longer available for other kinds of work, at least for a period of time. Priorities get set, and not everybody gets the number one slot.

To some extent, a project is like a mini-company running alongside your existing organization. That mini-company, like all growing organizations, needs entrepreneurial leadership.

Project leaders aren't always the same as project managers, in the same way that in a play the director is usually not the stage manager. The project as a whole needs leadership. The administration of a large, complex project needs someone to focus on the tracking and operations — a COO to the project manager's CEO. The BKPM, by the nature of the role, is the CEO.

Like any executive, the project manager views the project from a multifunctional perspective: operations, sales and marketing, finance, human resources, procurement, and the rest. The broader the frame of reference, the more effective the BKPM tends to be. Former executives often make great BKPMs because of that broad perspective, although this isn't universally true.

Businesses worry about customer and staff. This brings us back to the three-sided table. The BKPM manages customer relations and also manages the staff. That's why the BKPM must keep at a professional distance between them.

Process and Planning

If the strategic level of the project is the domain of leadership, the operational part of the project is project management. In the BKPM method, the key to project management is *balance*.

As we've said, the project charter is the written statement that brings together outcome, technical solution, and constraints. The project plan is the roadmap of the process — how we'll get from where we are to where we want to be.

While the basic steps are similar for almost every project, the level of detail and formality varies, all the way from back-of-the-envelope to full-bore project planning. Our key questions are these:

- What's actually in this project?
- What are we going to do?
- What *aren't* we going to do?

The BKPM must get agreement on the scope of the project, and break down the scope in sufficient detail so that the team can accomplish it. The initial high-level scope is usually part of the project charter agreement, but details often come later.

The traditional tool for breaking down scope is called a Work Breakdown Structure (WBS). While there's software available to handle this, a set of Post-it® notes are often all you need.

In a WBS, you prepare an "organizational chart" of the actual work packages that need to be accomplished. This both defines the work and helps the BKPM organize it. The big requirement of a WBS is that it contains *all* the work (and no more) that is necessary to achieve the outcome. Figure 4-2 provides an example.

Figure 4-2. Work Breakdown Structure. The Work Breakdown Structure (WBS) shows the work to be done in an organization chart format.

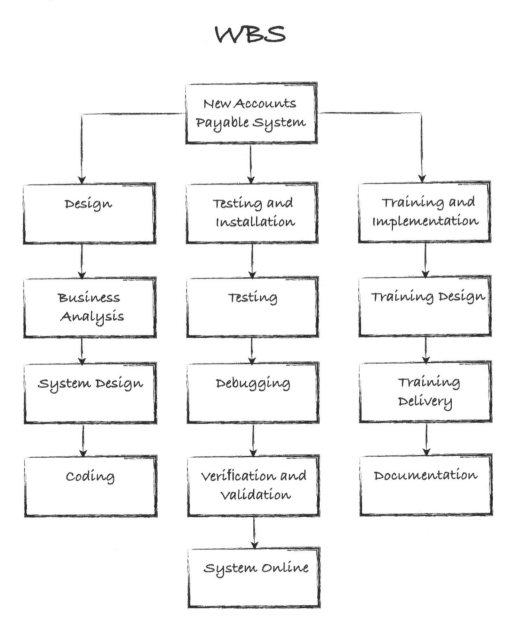

Each work package in the WBS will take a certain amount of time and consume a certain amount of resources. Putting that together gives us the schedule (Gantt chart, milestone chart, or a simple calendar), the budget (costs assigned to each element, usually a spreadsheet), and a list of work requirements for the BKPM to oversee and manage.

Once you've prepared the planning documents, wrap them into a project deck and hold a project kick-off meeting with the key team members to show them what they've asked you to undertake.

A good kick-off meeting is a powerful tool in the BKPM toolbox. It's an opportunity to build enthusiasm and commitment, a way to find out if there are serious doubts or concerns, and above all, a process to ensure that everyone starts the project on the same page.

Risk and Change

Managing risk and managing change are two of the most dangerous issues on any project. The BKPM must do an outstanding job of anticipating and planning for known risks, preparing for unknown risks, and for managing the inevitable changes that occur on any project.

Risk Management

Because project managers don't have crystal balls (although BKPMs need steel ones), we have risk management. When we look to the future, we may have a fairly good idea what is likely to happen, but if we think we know everything, we're deluding ourselves.

The goal of risk management isn't to predict the future. That's a mug's game. Instead, risk management is about trying to increase your chances of positive results.

Risks can be both negative (threats) and positive (opportunities). A *pure risk* only contains a threat. If we don't have an accident, our life continues on the way it was before. *Business risk* combines threat and opportunity. If we release a new product to market, we might make a lot of money, but the product may turn out to be a dog and we could lose a lot of money.

It's generally smart to avoid or limit pure risk as long as the price is right. We can buy insurance, implement safety standards, or generally act more prudently. But with business risk, the strategy changes. Sometimes, we want to *add* business risk to a project because we think we have a good chance at getting the upside result.

The fundamental formula for risk is R = P x I: the value of a risk is the probability of an event occurring times the impact of the event if it does occur. If there's a ten percent chance that we'll be late on a delivery, and the penalty is $1 million for being late, the value of the risk is 10% x $1 million, or $100,000. If we can eliminate the risk for less than $100,000, we are ahead of the game.

With a business risk, we add together the value of the risk for the downside and for the upside. If there's a ten percent chance of losing $4 million and a corresponding ninety percent chance of making $2 million, the expected value of the risk is (90% x $2,000,000) + (10% x -$4,000,000), which works out to $1.8 million - $400,000, or $1.4 million. Even though there's a chance of losing twice as much as we could gain, the likelihood of a positive outcome is so much higher that we'd see this as a pretty good bet. That's assuming, of course, that losing $4 million won't put us out of business.

Notice that the dollars involved don't always tell the whole story. In our pure risk scenario, we decided that spending less than $100,000 to get rid of the 10% x $1,000,000 risk was a good investment. But what if the cost of getting rid of the risk is $110,000? In that case, you have to make a values judgment about the *risk premium*. Is paying an extra $10,000 a good investment? Your mileage may vary.

On the business risk, we might still pass on the investment even though its expected value is $1.4 million if the consequence of losing $4 million would be catastrophic. We buy car insurance even though there's a risk premium involved (after all, the insurance company has overhead and wants a profit) because most of us can't afford the cost of a terrible accident. The probability may be low, but the impact is very high. Risk calculations help frame a decision, but they don't make the decision for you. You still have to do that by yourself.

The problem for BKPMs is that we frequently don't have good information about how likely an event is, or sometimes even what the net impact might be. If there's a small chance of a terrible financial loss, you can't turn that into a neat dollar figure using P x I, but the calculation still applies.

What's "low" times "terrible"? It may be "catastrophic," or it might only be "serious." That may not be great information, but you still have to make a decision.

Some projects have relatively low levels of risk, but those projects frequently aren't headed by BKPMs. If the project is serious enough to call in the big guns, the chances are that the risks are equally serious.

The basic outline of managing project risks goes like this.

Figure 4-3. Risk Management Process. This six-step approach to project risk is a vital part of effective project management.

1. Identify the risks.

2. Study the risks to understand their nature, probability, and impact.

3. Decide what (if anything) you can or should do about specific risks.

4. Establish a contingency reserve of extra money or time to cope with general and unforeseen risks.

5. Modify your project plan based on your risk solutions.

6. Monitor the risks on your project and act as necessary to deal with new risks that crop up from time to time.

Some organizations already have established risk management protocols. In others, you may need to develop your own to cope with the risks on a given project. While this is valuable, don't go overboard. You need a level of risk management that corresponds to the real risk level, and to the rewards and consequences that can result from risk events.

BKPMs are risk takers, but never foolhardy. You can't be afraid of risks when you step out into the unknown of projects, but that doesn't mean you shouldn't be careful and well prepared. If you're not a risk taker, you probably won't climb a mountain. But if you climb a mountain, you'll spend a lot of money and time to get your safety gear in good shape, and you'll be careful on the ascent.

Change Management

Change itself does not kill projects. *Uncontrolled and unmanaged change* kills projects. Change is to some extent both natural and inevitable, and can result in an improved project outcome. For the BKPM to manage the process, however, the BKPM must have a change management approach and methodology agreed to and put in place before the project begins.

Changes can be voluntary or involuntary. Examples of involuntary change are changes that are required because a project has encountered a risk, surprise, or speed bump. Voluntary changes normally (but not always) come from the customer. Perhaps changes elsewhere in the organization have altered the desired outcome, or affected the constraints that surround the project. Some changes are subject to negotiation; others present themselves as cold, hard facts.

It's vital that changes be put in writing, signed by the customer, evaluated by the BKPM, and integrated into the process. That's true no matter what the change, where it comes from, how negotiable it is, or why it's being made. Any change that falls outside the process is a danger to the project.

Special Issues

Agile vs. Waterfall

There are always hot topics in management circles, from Six Sigma to "lean" methodologies. One of the big issues in recent project management has been the development of "agile" methods of running a project, as opposed to the traditional "waterfall" method. We discussed that a little earlier in this chapter when we talked about projects in which the customer isn't clear about the desired outcome or process. That's one situation that calls for agile thinking, but it's not the only one.

Some classes of projects have pretty clear outcomes, but the details need iterative development. In writing this book, for example, we did know the basic philosophy and approach even before a single word was written. However, the book had to iterate through a number of drafts to make sure the final product was clear and accurate.

In the waterfall method, tasks follow a rigid sequence of dependencies. Task B can't start until Task A is finished. If something delays Task A, the start of Task B is immediately in jeopardy. In agile, the situation is far more fluid. The project goes through iterations, in which a rough product becomes increasingly refined and robust. One task may not follow another in any rigid sense.

There are advantages and risks in both approaches, but advocates for each tend to oversell their virtues and downplay their faults. In most cases, we think an arbitrary preference of one method over another is a waste of time. The crucial question is this: *What is the simplest way forward?*

Initiatives vs. Projects

Projects, by definition, *end*. That's in contrast to operations, which are ongoing. In between the two, however, there's a gray area we'll call *initiatives*. Initiatives have some characteristics of projects and some characteristics of operations. If you're implementing a lean Six Sigma initiative, for example, there's definitely a need for a plan and a kick-off meeting, but the initiative doesn't have a crisp, clear end point.

The most important difference to consider is that in an initiative, action is more important than outcomes. In our hypothetical lean Six Sigma initiative, you have to push forward, but without a defined end point, any progress is good. Situational awareness and clarity of thought matter more than a detailed plan.

The Learning Customer

One place to prefer agile over waterfall development is when you have a "learning customer." The learning customer can't specify everything clearly up front, although the customer usually has an idea about the desired end state.

There are many legitimate reasons why this might be the case. For example, perhaps no one knows the underlying situation well enough to know what issues or opportunities may arise. In an overall initiative, the learning customer is the norm, not the exception. Initiatives are big and complex, they have multiple stakeholders with different interests and points of view, and seemingly innocuous changes can have unpredictable ripple effects.

In this case, an iterative approach is the best you can do. Agree on an interim goal, manage the team to accomplish it, and then go over it with the customer. How close are you? What have you learned? Are you done, or do you need to do more work?

In the old Total Quality Management (TQM) approach, popular in the 1980s and 1990s, the mantra was "continuous improvement," an iterative way to improve quality. To manage quality improvement, TQM guru W. Edwards Deming used the PDCA cycle: Plan, Do, Check, Act, shown in Figure 4-4.

Figure 4-4. PDCA Cycle. From quality to iterative projects, the PDCA Cycle is a powerful approach to achieving continuous improvement goals.

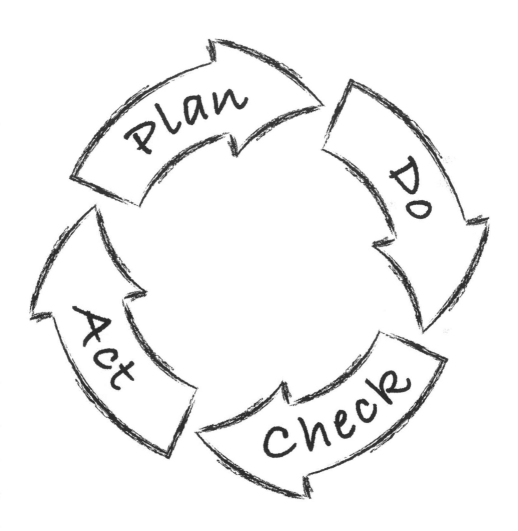

- **Plan:** Develop a plan based on available knowledge and understanding.

- **Do:** Execute the plan as well as possible.

- **Check:** Evaluate what you've done; identify problems and issues along with root causes and areas for improvement.

- **Act:** Decide on the next step. Are you done? How has your knowledge changed? What should you do next?

Lather, rinse, repeat.

5

Why Projects Fail — and How BKPM Prevents It

The CHAOS Report Revisited

THE CHAOS REPORT, as we learned earlier, showed that nearly three quarters of all projects could be considered failures. Failures, in the CHAOS Report, describe projects that were either cancelled before completion or that didn't meet at least one of the Triple Constraints — they were late, over budget, or didn't meet all the performance requirements.

Nobody *wants* to fail. Unfortunately, as the CHAOS Report tells us, most projects *do* fail, either in whole or in part. No system, no matter how good, can prevent every failure. But a good system can reduce both the *frequency* and the *severity* of failure.

The CHAOS Report grouped projects into three "resolution types." Here are their definitions.

- **Failed.** The project is cancelled before completion.

- **Challenged.** The project is completed and operational, but over-budget, over the time estimate, and with fewer features and functions than initially specified.

- **Successful.** The project is completed on time and on budget, with all features and functions as originally specified.

From a technical point of view, those categories make sense, but from a customer-centered point of view, things look very different indeed.

The Virtue of Failed Projects

Let's start with *failed*. That means the project was cancelled before completion. Is that necessarily a bad thing? If you're attempting a risky project, you may want to look ahead to see if there are any "go/no-go" decision points. Canceling a project before it goes off the rails can save a fortune — and make risks more worth taking. After all, organizational success is built on the idea that we do the things valuable to the organization, not waste money on projects that should never have been started to begin with.

In fact, one of the most important roles of the BKPM is to *force early failure*. If a project's wrong-headed, destined to fail, too expensive, not worth the risk, or otherwise problematic, killing the project before it gets underway is arguably a good thing. It saves money, avoids damage to organizational (and individual) reputations, and above all, allows the organization and the customer to discover the *right* project, and do that instead.

Don't you want your project manager to tell you when that's the case? Failure, in this sense, should be considered a victory for everyone concerned. Failing early is dramatically cheaper and better than failing late, after all the money, time, and effort has been sunk.

The BKPM's role at the beginning of any project is to determine if the goals are clear and doable, the budget and resources are sufficient, and the implementation team is capable of performing the necessary work. If that's not the case, either the situation has to change or the project needs to stop then and there until the situation is resolved.

One might argue that the highest order of business for a BKPM is preventing project failure. Whether the project never leaves the docks (stopped before the failure can be damaging) or makes it to the New World (achieves meaningful success even if the success isn't what was originally defined), by hook or by crook the BKPM can say, "Yes, that was ugly – but we designed it that way." This is a powerful statement indeed.

When you stack up the cost of hiring an outstanding BKPM against the cost of letting an ill-conceived project burn through money and resources, it's clear that no matter how much a BKPM costs (and they don't come cheap), it's a bargain.

When "Challenged" Is Just Another Word for Nothing Left to Lose

Challenged has both positive and negative connotations. Sometimes, "challenged" becomes a politically correct term for "screwed." Some aspect of the triple constraint, whether it's time, cost, performance (or all three), has been compromised.

There's usually a small window in which that's no problem. If your $30 million construction project ends up $250,000 over budget (a little less than one percent), depending on the circumstances, people aren't likely to be that upset. But outside that window, you've got trouble.

In another sense, however, "challenged" is a good thing. A challenged project, after all, is challenging — and going after a stretch goal may be worth it even if you fall short. Take, for example, the infamous Denver International Airport (DIA) project, which opened 16 months behind schedule and nearly $2 billion over budget.

Widely derided as a project management failure, today DIA is the 5th busiest airport in the world measured by aircraft movements. It has been voted Best Airport in North America by *Business Traveler* magazine six years in a row, and *Time* called it "America's Best Run Airport" in 2002.

As embarrassing and damaging as the cost and schedule overruns were, Denver is probably still a lot better off than it would have been without the new airport, and over the long lifetime of an operating airport, it's still likely to deliver a net economic benefit, if one slightly slower in coming than initially planned.

Of course, everyone involved would have preferred that these problems not happen, but with a project that massive, the idea that *nothing* would go wrong was simply ludicrous. "Failure" must be kept in perspective.

It can easily be argued that just about every project of significant scope is at least potentially challenged — fraught with the kinds of risks that cause problems: unclear costs, political issues, fuzzy objectives, problematic technology. That doesn't necessarily argue for project cancellation, but we must be conscious of risks before stepping into any project.

Fake "Success"

Even projects the CHAOS Report would define as "successful" can sometimes mislead. That's what happens when, contrary to every bit of available evidence, the organization persists in claiming that the project has actually succeeded.

Microsoft once claimed that the Zune was successful. Apple trumpeted its success with the Newton. Coca-Cola proclaimed that with the release of New Coke, it had won the Cola Wars. Often, there's some temporary factor that they can cite in favor of their claim, but it's generally clear to the rest of the world that this is bullshit — at least in the long run.

These examples also demonstrate that an organization can fool itself into believing almost anything it wants. This is particularly true when the CEO or top leadership invests ego in the decision. Executives too often believe they control the outside universe as strongly as they control their own organizations, and end up forcing everyone else to drink the Kool-Aid.

Fake success can also result from stopping too soon. If you sell your stock when it goes up a few cents in value, you make some money, but if the stock skyrockets in value over the next six months, you left a whole lot of money on the table. Just because you got where you originally decided to go doesn't mean you went far enough.

That's one more argument in favor of the BKPM and the three-sided table. Someone has to have the courage and organizational position to say that the Emperor, in fact, has no clothes — or conversely, that the Emperor is overdressed.

Success is in some ways subjective, and so is failure. This subjectivity requires an argument for defining meaningful success. That's also why CEOs of entrepreneurial endeavors (a category which clearly includes BKPMs) don't just stop at the first failure. They learn, improve, justify, and move forward. The CHAOS approach isn't necessarily wrong, but it's not complete. Project ownership requires that you *measure the right thing* — and the "right thing" is different on different projects.

N-Dimensional Failure

Of course, there are real failures in project management, but they often require the BKPM to put the project in a wider context and to look deep beneath the surface to see what's really going on. Failures, you see, are seldom one-dimensional.

Projects are normally multidimensional. Measuring project success (and, for that matter, failure) can cover cost, time, performance, risk, quality, return on investment, regulatory compliance, degree of improvement, and more.

While we'd sooner not fail at any of these, sometimes failure in one area strengthens another. Depending on relative priority and value, it may be very much in the interest of the project to choose some failures if they result in other successes. While technically a failure, we could equally argue that it was a net improvement — as in the case of DIA.

There is almost a Darwinian dynamic that occurs in these situations when the organization obtains the real improvement benefits from the project, even when they differ from the theoretical or imagined benefits. It takes the wider organizational perspective of a BKPM to recognize and articulate these kinds of successes — instead of letting them be unfairly labeled as failures.

As we learned in our discussion of the hierarchy of constraints, the project must achieve the driver, but has increasing flexibility in the weak constraint. If you miss the deadline, on one project it's not a big deal, and on the other, you're dead. Same thing with cost and performance.

If the performance is paramount, and you have a problem, you probably should spend extra money. If it's not, you're better off dropping some features on your wish list.

But the bottom line is this — are you better off having done the project than you would have been if you didn't do it at all?

Types of Real Failure — and What To Do About Them

While some failures (and some successes) are imaginary, others are all too real. Let's look at the sources of failure and how the BKPM should deal with each.

Mistakes

One obvious cause of project failure, it would seem, is mistakes.

Actually, that's not the case. Mistakes (as such) are seldom the problem. After all, mistakes are natural and inevitable. Because projects are complex, constrained, and unique, mistake-free projects are the exception, not the norm.

If something is inevitable on your project, it constitutes a *known risk*. If you fail to plan for it, that's your failure as a project manager, not the failure of the person making a mistake.

Even on a nuclear submarine you can't afford to assume no one will ever make a mistake. Therefore, you add safety controls, checks and balances, and other systems to catch and correct those mistakes either before they happen or at least before they produce any bad effects.

Mistakes aren't all created equal. Some mistakes, if made, could sink the project; others are barely noticeable. Some mistakes are both rare and difficult to make; others are all too easy.

Depending on the severity and the ease of a particular mistake, it's incumbent upon the BKPM to ensure that adequate mechanisms are in place to control for natural error. It's part of the process.

When mistakes slip through your system, the issue to address is the system, not the mistake itself. You can't change the past; you can only affect the present and the future. The challenge is keeping the problem from happening a second time. Figure 5-1 identifies strategies for managing mistakes.

Figure 5-1. Mistake Management

1. Catch mistakes early, before they have a chance to cascade out of control.

2. Don't shame people for making mistakes; it only encourages people to hide them.

3. Identify any critical areas where mistakes can be most damaging, and put in extra checks and balances.

4. Identify areas that are fault-tolerant, where less than perfect is plenty good enough, and favor speed over perfection in getting those done.

5. Build some inefficiency into the plan.

6. Look for the root cause of mistakes. Some are the result of carelessness, others the result of inadequate training or support.

7. Separate the person from the problem, but pay attention to both. Assume good intent and attitude on the part of the mistake-maker; that's usually right. Few mistakes are deliberate or passive-aggressive — and if they are, it will become clear soon enough.

Execution, by and large, doesn't have to be flawless, but rather good enough to get the job done. Overemphasis on preventing minor mistakes tends to bog the project down in "analysis paralysis," where no one wants to act for fear of being blamed if things don't go perfectly. Fault tolerance speeds project success.

Failure of Vision/Wrong Vision

The most critical project failures can almost always be traced back to issues with the vision.

Failure of vision means the failure to define a clear vision in the first place. Perhaps the customer or client doesn't understand his or her own needs completely. Sometimes there's ego involved, or a fear of appearing ignorant, or even an attempt to shift responsibility for the lack of results.

Other times, the vision is clear, but wrong. Wrong visions are ones that won't solve the underlying issue, even if they are successfully implemented. Wrong visions are misunderstanding of the problem, or misunderstanding of what solutions are or are not possible. Wrong visions are misunderstanding about root causes, human motivations, or organizational issues.

Unchallenged visions haven't been tested or analyzed enough to know if they're right or wrong. They have lots of hidden assumptions. Unchallenged visions haven't been tested to see if their cost and time projections are reasonable. Unchallenged visions may signify customers who don't want to face their own problems head on.

All these kinds of vision problems can destroy projects.

In the three-sided table, as we've learned, the customer or client is responsible for the vision of the project, but it's the

BKPM's job to make sure it's done and done properly. If there's a problem with the vision, the scope is either vague or wrong, and the budget and schedule, accordingly, are based on false premises. In the end, we can only choose among spending more money, taking more time, or doing less — whichever hurts least.

Failures of vision belong first and foremost to the customer or client, but it's the BKPM's job to make sure that doesn't happen, even if it means pushing back or confronting the client. Better to have the fight now instead of waiting until you've spent all the money and missed the deadline before you agree what the actual project is all about.

As we noted earlier, a vision can evolve, so don't assume just because there's no vision at the outset that there won't be any vision at the end. Help educate your client or customer when it's best to allow a vision to develop iteratively.

Figure 5-2. Without Vision, the Project Perishes

1. The single most important thing you can do as a BKPM is to apply costs to proposed visions to help customers see the consequences of their choices.

2. Ask what other options have been considered. If none have, consider some.

3. Ask what the ideal situation will look like if the problem is solved completely.

4. Ask if it would still be worth doing if it took twice as long or cost twice as much.

Changing Vision

Change doesn't kill projects. Unplanned and unmanaged change kills projects.

In the realm of changes, change orders, and modified projects, we distinguish between ordinary technical changes and the sort of change that modifies the overall vision, rather than just the technical dimension itself.

There are various reasons why a project vision can change or evolve. If there's a research and development (R&D) component to what you are doing, you're naturally going to discover some things you didn't expect. This may require adjusting the vision of your project.

Sometimes external circumstances force a change in vision. Economic assumptions may change. The competitive environment may alter. Technological breakthroughs can happen.

In all these cases, what's real is real, even when it's not convenient. Although the project has now changed in important and material ways and the goalposts have moved considerably, this kind of evolutionary change isn't the same thing as a failure of the project. It may even be an improvement.

Because this kind of change cannot easily be controlled, you can find yourself far from where you started, with resources, budget, and deadline structured around the original (obsolete) objective.

If there's reason to believe your project vision is likely to evolve (R&D, competitive environment, fast-moving technology), structure the project with the idea of change in mind. Build in flexibility of schedule and budget so that you can respond to inevitable change without driving the project off its rails. Drive an understanding of the likelihood of change with the other sides of the three-sided table so that they will be ready and prepared when change is required.

Using the three-sided table approach, the BKPM must work with project sponsors/customers and technical team members to accommodate and adapt to change — even (or especially) in circumstances where one or both are likely to be resistant. Project customers may be reluctant to accept the ways reality has changed. Implementation teams resist throwing away work products, even if they're no longer relevant to the modified goal.

Directional projects are ok, although they are often better as initiatives, not projects. But it is possible to structure an initiative with a discrete set of goals, budget, and timeline, using an iterative process.

In one large IT project, we structured the project in phases. The first phase focused on achieving an understanding of the issues, problems, and circumstances, leading to clarity in the second phase, and further refinement in the third phase. Because the object of the project was progress in the right direction, both BKPM and client considered this a success even though the outcome never achieved the initial vision.

In this project, frankly, the initial vision was ridiculous, and everyone but the outcome owner could see this. However, the outcome owner wanted the project pursued, and they had the money and control.

How can you argue against this? The simple bottom line is that you can't! To put a project like this into the BKPM model, you must *frame* the project so that the lack of vision/wrong vision combined with the desire to pursue an impossible objective turns from inevitable failure to an iterative search for success.

Unknown Unknowns

Everyone in project management knows the famous quote by former Secretary of Defense Donald Rumsfeld. "[A]s we know, there are known knowns; there are things we know we know. We also know there are known unknowns; that is to say we know there are some things we do not know. But there are also unknown unknowns—the ones we don't know we don't know."

While Rumsfeld came under a lot of criticism for this point, it's actually a well-known axiom in risk management. Some risks are "known knowns." We understand the risk, we know the probability, we can measure the impact, and there is no excuse for not being prepared.

"Known unknowns" are situations in which we are aware of specific gaps in our knowledge and understanding. We don't know what the competition is about to release, or what new breakthrough in technology is going to happen, but we are aware that these kinds of surprises do happen. We can prepare for these kinds of risks even in the absence of having all the data.

"Unknown unknowns" are the risks we aren't aware of on any level. If they happen, they're likely to come as a complete surprise. How can we prepare for this kind of situation? There are actually a number of potential strategies.

Figure 5-3. Managing Unknown Unknowns

1. Be aware that unknown unknowns are out there, and that they can disrupt your project. Stay alert to signs and signals that suggest that a surprise is in the offing.

2. Don't commit all your resources in advance. Keep a reserve handy.

3. Adopt a three-dimensional approach. After all, anything that happens can only have three types of impact on your project: make you late, drive up your cost, or drive down your performance. If you have strategies for recovery in all three dimensions, it matters a whole lot less what the surprise actually is.

4. Dig deeper. Some "unknown unknowns" are only unknown because we haven't looked hard enough.

Interestingly, Donald Rumsfeld missed one more possibility. In addition to known knowns, known unknowns, and unknown unknowns, don't fall for *unknown knowns*.

These are issues you really *do* know, but for some reason are blind to them.

Assuming that the client knows what he or she wants, that team members don't have any agendas of their own, or that everyone understands a situation the same way can get you into trouble. Too often, the truth is right in front of our eyes, but we don't see it.

Various cognitive biases can interfere with your ability to see what's clearly there. Look out for such problems as the ambiguity aversion effect, in which people prefer a decision that's less ambiguous over a decision that's clearly better; confirmation bias, in which we focus only on facts that support what we already believe; or the famous Hawthorne Effect, in which almost any change triggers at least some temporary improvement just because people feel someone's paying attention. (You can download a free encyclopedia of cognitive biases from http://efanzines.com/RandomJottings/RandomJottings06.pdf.)

Becoming a
Bare-Knuckled
Project Manager

The Evolution of a Bare-Knuckled Project Manager

N O ONE starts out as a BKPM. A BKPM has skills and abilities born of experience, and you have to earn — and learn from — the experience.

In fact, very few people start out in life looking to become project managers in the first place. In many ways, it's an accidental profession — good project managers are drafted into the field.

That's true even in the current world, where some colleges and universities offer degrees in project management, and the industry organizations are talking about project management career paths. Most of us learn to manage projects based on the technical or business field where we start out. IT professionals learn to manage IT projects. Construction workers become construction project managers. Financial professionals learn to manage financial projects.

You'll hear that any competent project manager can manage any sort of project — whether or not he or she has subject matter experience. There's some truth in that, but not a whole lot.

Figure 6-1. The BKPM Zone. The growth pattern of project managers starts with novice PMs and grows to master PMs — but true Bare-Knuckled Project Managers are few. They are the best of the best.

You can certainly manage a project without being an expert in the topic, but there's usually a minimum you have to know in order to be effective. Of course, some parts of project management are generic enough that experience in one field helps you manage projects in another, but that's never quite as good.

As you reach executive levels in project management — the levels where BKPMs come into play — the problem changes. Projects at this level often cut across many functional lines and involve specialists with diverse backgrounds. As a BKPM, you may know some of the fields, but you're unlikely to know them all. Or you take on a project not because you're the recognized expert, but rather because you're the only leader available for the job.

How, then, do you become a BKPM? What are the steps and stages in the BKPM's career progression? Normally, there are a series of stages in a project manager's career:

- **"Working" Project Manager** (part-time project manager, full-time technical specialist)
- **Junior Project Manager** (managing one or more simultaneous projects, usually small in size)
- **Journeyman Project Manager** (trained and usually certified in project management, knows the fundamentals and has reasonable experience)
- **Master Project Manager** (skilled and experienced, knows the field, may or may not be a great leader)
- **Bare-Knuckled Project Manager** (a trained, capable, and effective leader who gets the job done)

"Working" Project Manager

At the beginning of your rise in the project management hierarchy, you're often what we call a "working" project manager. That means you simultaneously serve as a technical resource on the project as well as the project manager. This sets up a conflict.

Notice that the PMI approach presumes that if you're the project manager, that's your whole job. It's not an unreasonable position to take. Project management normally takes more time and involvement than anyone suspects when the project begins. In the real world, however, it's usually the case that new project managers don't have that luxury. As a result, certain problems are all too common.

Self-bottlenecking. Too often, the inexperienced PM decides that he or she is the most competent technical team member (which may well be true; that's probably why he or she got appointed to the job in the first place) and should therefore take on the toughest technical challenges. This almost always backfires, because you become your own technical bottleneck, consumed with your own work and thus unable to help the rest of your team.

Lack of independent perspective. In the three-sided table model, the project manager must be separate from the implementation team. When the PM is also a member of the working group, the three-sided table is corrupted right from the start.

Lack of training and experience. Newly minted project managers of this stripe seldom get much (if anything) in the way of training or coaching, and may not know the simplest of project management tools. This creates a lack of confidence, compounded by a lack of fundamental skills. Some organizations provide a Project Management Office (PMO) to support these project managers, while others expect them to somehow learn on the job.

Junior Project Manager

Minted, but not yet honed, junior project managers usually have just enough project management knowledge to be dangerous. While technical skills may be extremely high, practical experience in the ins-and-outs of projects is often lacking. Junior project managers may have been to an introductory project management class or two, but seldom have any meaningful hands-on experience with the process.

Whether a junior project manager will mature into a fully capable BKPM has more to do with attitude and personality than with mastery of the technical minutiae of project management. This isn't to say, of course, that there isn't value in learning the technical fundamentals, but rather that they aren't enough. An outstanding project manager can always find someone to keep the project books.

Common problems with junior project managers revolve around ownership and overload.

Grabbing for control. The desire for control often manifests itself most strongly when people feel a general lack of control, and that's a common characteristic of a junior project manager. Feeling threatened and disrespected, a junior PM may be too aggressive, taking ownership for things they do not — and should not — own.

Too many projects. At the junior PM level, projects are relatively small, and it's often not economically feasible to have one PM for one project. Multiple project management becomes inevitable. Multiple projects are, however, more complex than a single project of the same total scope and budget. Different customers, different priorities, and resource conflicts eat away at any attempt to control.

Seizing up. When the level and complexity of work gets too large for someone to handle, the natural reaction is to seize up under the collapsing pressure of owning too much. This leads to forgotten and abandoned projects, with neglect driving some projects out of existence.

Journeyman Project Manager

In recent years, there's been a move to professionalize project management. We've talked about PMI's PMP® designation, based on understanding the PMBOK® approach to project management. Universities offer undergraduate and graduate degrees in project management. Numerous training organizations offer certificates of their own.

These types of credentials show that the person has at least a minimum level of competence and a reasonable amount of actual experience in project management. That's important, but it's not enough. What none of the credentials do, however, is demonstrate whether or not the *person* has the temperament, drive, and style to be effective in the rough-and-tumble world of projects. That's the difference between a well-qualified project manager and a BKPM.

Many project managers are comfortable staying at this level, managing relatively repetitive projects in an increasingly familiar field. They have a reasonable batting average, but they're definitely playing in the minor leagues with no particular desire to move forward.

Often, project management offices (PMO) are set up to provide technical oversight and support of individual projects, lessening the need for large numbers of trained and qualified project managers. Journeyman PMs are often drafted for this role. They have the technical expertise in project management, but may not have the leadership ability to run large projects themselves.

A well-run PMO can be of significant benefit to an organization, but there are common problems resulting from the preponderance of journeyman project managers.

Overconfidence. The PMP® credential all by itself tells you very little about whether a project manager is competent or not. It merely tells you that the PM in question has a command of certain basic tools and procedures. Nevertheless, a PM in possession of a new credential may take on a level of arrogance completely inappropriate to the actual accomplishment, and start acting as if the PMO is the owner, subject matter expert, and Supreme High Factotum for every active project.

Process over Product. The formal project management process is elaborate and comprehensive, but as we've learned, it can easily be overkill based on the nature of a given project. Credentialed PMs may emphasize the formal process regardless whether it's the right tool for the situation.

Master Project Manager

There are project managers with substantial experience and ability who don't quite measure up to the BKPM standard. While highly competent in many respects, these "master project managers" have a command of their subject area but sometimes lack both the executive leadership ability and the broader perspective necessary for peak performance.

Master PMs normally have a good technical background, not merely in the subject matter of the project, but also in the discipline of project management. This can include the PMP® or similar credentials, but training in such topics as Six Sigma, Agile methodology, or almost any substantial technical management discipline can work. Many master PMs have credentials in more than one of these areas. However, the presence of credentials doesn't make someone a master PM, and the absence of credentials doesn't prove someone isn't.

For large but routine projects, master project managers know how to keep the system moving forward. They are well organized, detail oriented, prudent, and generally effective. For that reason, master PMs often get assigned responsibility for managing the PMO. This is often a good use of talent, because the master PM is an operations officer, not an executive one.

It is when things deviate from the standard that trouble is in the offing. At the beginning of this book, we cited the CHAOS Report findings that the majority of large projects fail. These projects generally are not managed by junior staff, but rather by project managers with significant experience — and yet they still fail. Common problems with master project managers include the following.

Difficulty confronting the customer. The traditional saying "The customer is always right" doesn't always work where projects are concerned. As we discussed in the three-sided table, the project manager must be willing to push the client or customer just as hard as the implementation team. Master project managers are comfortable pushing the implementation team, but when it comes to the customer, they are less willing to confront defective vision and to tell the customer up front when the proposed project is likely to fail.

Thinking Inside the Box. Because the customer sets the master PM's direction and isn't subject to much challenge, the range of discretion and initiative available to the master PM is often limited. Answers are pursued within a relatively narrow span.

Owned by the System. When the organization uses a PMO to support its project managers, the PMO usually becomes part of the bureaucracy rather than a center for innovation and success. The PMO oversees the full range of projects, failures as well as successes, but usually doesn't have final P&L responsibility. Failure in this environment is usually well documented, but that doesn't automatically translate into improvement.

Bare-Knuckled Project Manager

There may not be much of a difference in the education and credentials of a BKPM compared to a master PM, but there's a world of practical difference. While BKPMs typically rise through the ranks, what distinguishes a BKPM is *leadership*. All the textbooks and credentials in the world aren't enough.

As most of us know, no matter how technically challenging the project, it's almost always the people and political issues that take up the project manager's time and keep him or her up at night. No classroom or certificate can teach you how to handle that part of the job. It not only takes a high level of skill to navigate the political seas, it also takes gravitas — the respect you get from experience, temperament, and confidence. It takes a certain number of years and more than a few scars to achieve this level.

Using the three-sided table approach, the BKPM is a partner of the customer / client, not a subordinate. By managing the interaction between customer and implementation team, the BKPM is in a position to ensure a project's success in a way that other project managers can only dream about. Some of the specific qualifications and qualities of the BKPM that lead to success include the following.

Honest Broker. The BKPM does not and cannot drink the corporate Kool-Aid. This can be uncomfortable for some executives who aren't used to being challenged, but this attitude is for everyone's good. The BKPM is an arm's-length strategist — he or she does not take a side. This independence allows the BKPM to serve as a referee when necessary, and to serve as an objective analysis.

Executive/Fighter. By their very nature, executives own the problems and issues in their portfolio. Working with substantial independence and initiative, they chart and lead the path to success. Of course, if a problem is easy, it's usually already been solved. A BKPM, as we've learned, is also a fighter, able to face and overcome the myriad obstacles that stand between success and ourselves.

Unleashing Your Inner BKPM

The standard for becoming a BKPM is very high. You need experience, command of the process, credibility, courage, and honesty. All of these things take time, and even then, not everyone internalizes these qualities.

To add to the challenge, BKPMs must also approach the job with an appropriate level of humility. We are, after all, pressed into the service of others. Keeping ego out of the process, focusing on results, and not seeking power for its own sake all help separate the BKPM from the normal range of executives.

Not seeking power for its own sake isn't the same thing as not seeking — and exercising — power as appropriate. However, the real power of a BKPM is the power that comes from respect, as measured by results.

You need to approach the project with an open mind. The plan is simply a baseline. It has little to do with reality. That's why the project manager needs to think like a martial artist, seeing the subtle movements in the project environment and choosing the right response.

You need commitment. You must take ownership of the process. You have the responsibility of making the goals and objective clear, even when parties resist being pinned down. You must oversee and validate the technical solution, and make an independent judgment about the likelihood of meeting the triple constraints.

Imagine the benefits to the organization when that kind of person manages your toughest projects. Risk goes down, accountability and control go up. The organization actually improves as a result. You have an honest broker to keep open communication between the customer and the team. You get sound advice and alternative options. And all that helps you get a good night's sleep.

The BKPM should be a highly compensated individual — just like *Pulp Fiction's* Winston Wolf.

(He drives an NSX.)

Personality Styles of the BKPM

We've talked about Bruce Lee, General George S. Patton, and a few other famous figures that embody the traits of a BKPM. But what if you're not like that? Are BKPMs limited to a very few personality types, or can different people aspire to reach the level of a true bare-knuckled project manager?

We believe that there's more than one way to reach the highest pinnacles of success. General Patton — loud, brash, hard charging, and effective — was a BKPM, but so was his boss, General Eisenhower. Although Eisenhower was much less flashy, he was no less driven and goal-oriented. Both men got the job done in spite of tremendous obstacles. What distinguishes a BKPM isn't a particular personality style, but a way of doing business.

There are many tools used to classify personality and temperament types, from DiSC to the Myers-Briggs Type Indicator (MBTI), but those are a bit too complex for everyday practical use. Instead, let's use a simpler, more classic approach, with four easily identifiable types that represent the vast majority of people. Figure 6-2 shows how this works.

Figure 6-2. Personality Types and the BKPM. Check the words that describe you. Many people have elements of all four groups, but most of us have a dominant work style. What's yours?

Direct

FOCUSER	**INTEGRATOR**
POSITIVE	POSITIVE
Determined	Imaginative
Controlled	Creative
Commanding	Energetic
Authoritative	Future-Directed
NEGATIVE	NEGATIVE
Domineering	Unrealistic
Autocratic	Manic
Hard-Headed	Unable to finish
Tyrannical	Poor time management
OPERATOR	**RELATER**
POSITIVE	POSITIVE
Detailed	Listener
Accurate	Team Player
Organized	Loyal
Methodical	Sympathetic
NEGATIVE	NEGATIVE
Obsessive	Unassertive
Rigid	Conforming
Compulsive	Gushing
Slow	Indecisive

Task

People

Indirect

We're sure you recognize all four of these types from your everyday life. If you have trouble spotting them (or trouble classifying yourself), here's a simple method. Notice that the two axes of the grid are **Task → People** and **Direct → Indirect.**

Figure 6-2 summarizes the characteristics of each. You can determine your personality style according to this model — or make a good guess about somebody else — by observing certain key behavior. The "Rating Temperament" exercise helps you make this determination quickly and easily.

Rating Temperament

To determine your temperament type (or the type of someone else), rate your opinion of how the person in question reflects the described characteristic.

Directness

Direct people tend to be fast-paced, say what they mean, and be more naturally assertive. They make quick decisions. They are often more likely to interrupt or "talk on top of" other speakers.

Low				High
1	2	3	4	5

Indirectness

Indirect people tend to have a slower conversational pace, listen first and talk second, and provide background first before getting to the point. They usually wait until there's a real gap in the conversation before speaking up.

Low   High

1   2   3   4   5

Task Orientation

Task-oriented people show their emotions less, focus on tasks and goals, and spend less focus on relationships and people.

Low   High

1   2   3   4   5

People Orientation

People-oriented people tend to express emotional reactions and feeling easily and openly, and believe relationships and people are important in the work environment.

Low   High

1   2   3   4   5

Scoring and Application

Direct and Task-Oriented	=	**Focuser**
Indirect and Task-Oriented	=	**Operator**
Direct and People-Oriented	=	**Integrator**
Indirect and People-Oriented	=	**Relater**

No one style is the "right" style. Everyone has natural strengths and weaknesses. When it comes to work:

Focusers get the job done no matter what obstacles stand in their way — but sometimes leave a swath of damage in their wake.

Integrators are natural brainstormers and problem solvers with a never-ending supply of ideas — but don't always follow through.

Operators are great planners and naturally detail oriented — but can get bogged down in the small stuff.

Relaters are great team builders and excellent motivators — but can get so wrapped up in the people that they lose track of the goal.

In other words, everybody has advantages…and everybody has disadvantages. BKPMs can come from any of the four types, but through hard work, maturity, focus, and self-awareness they have managed to limit their weak spots and extend their abilities past their own style to be versatile no matter the situation.

Some people are hybrids, carrying the strengths and weaknesses of more than one category. Some even exhibit one style at the office and a completely different one at home.

Clearly, all four sets of skills and aptitudes are valuable for an organization. Great BKPMs are versatile. Even though we all start with a preference, that doesn't mean we can't learn to do effectively what may not always be natural.

You can use temperament for self-examination: determine your strengths and weaknesses and gain insight into how you can improve. In mentoring others, you can identify where another person may need support.

To lead others more effectively, pay attention to their style. People tend to think their own style is natural, so if you move your behavior in their direction, you're more likely to get results. If you are dealing with a direct person, be more direct; with an indirect person, slow down. With task-oriented people, focus on the task; with people-oriented types, focus on relationships.

Great leaders always grow themselves and the people around them. The BKPM leaves people and organizations stronger than they were before.

Limbic Learning

Regular learning, however, can only take you so far. In our discussion of *Jeet Kune Do*, we remember that Bruce Lee said that combat was spontaneous. You can't predict it, but only react to it. That doesn't mean, however, that it isn't predictable or controllable.

The type of learning that allows you to react effortlessly and spontaneously doesn't come from books, seminars, or even from (normal) experience. It comes from *limbic learning*.

Good steel has to be forged. It's hammered, beaten, and melted into shape. It's stressed and edged and honed. All the qualities that make a good sword make a good BKPM. The way that's done is through the limbic system, the place where emotions live.

The limbic system is a small structure located in the middle of the brain, in between the brain stem and the cortex. The brain stem is the center of alertness and arousal, while the cortex is the home for most of our higher-level thinking and learning. Mediating between the two is the limbic system, home to human emotion.

This limbic system serves as a link and as a reinforcer. Purely intellectual learning doesn't change behavior enough all by itself. The limbic system must be involved for true change to take place.

How Limbic Learning Works

Former Special Forces interrogator Gregory Hartley describes the process of limbic learning this way:

> "Any condition that creates unease, restlessness, instability, and/or unpredictability…[causes you to] experience a temporary loss of control that may

overwhelm you. You lose your ability to function at your peak state because you move out of organized thought and into an emotional state, or limbic mode." (Hartley and Karinch, 26)

That's why top athletes and martial artists practice their sport or fighting skills under stress. As Hartley says, "When the time comes, their bodies automatically know what to do."

That's limbic learning in a nutshell, and it's the powerful and overwhelming quality that distinguishes the BKPM from other project managers. Projects, after all, operate in an environment of continual stress: unease, instability and unpredictability are the norm, not the exception.

No matter how technically competent you may be, if your learning lives only in your cortex and not in your limbic system, it won't be available to you under conditions of stress — exactly the time where you are most likely to need it.

The true learning of a BKPM comes not from the classroom, but from field experience. The ability to operate under these conditions can only be gained by experiencing these conditions, over and over again.

Regardless of temperament or personality type, what all BKPMs have in common is that they have learned to operate with the deep learning that is only possible when the limbic system is engaged.

If you've managed projects long enough, you've experienced the kinds of stress and uncertainty that trigger limbic mode, but not everyone is able to smooth the transition and make the learning permanent. If the stress becomes too much, your brain loses the ability to function logically.

When you're trying to develop the high performance leaders you need for your toughest projects, there's no substitute for stress. At the same time, you need to provide the support structure that keeps people from being overwhelmed. When you achieve that balance, deep learning takes place.

Every effective BKPM goes through this seasoning process not once, but many times over. Whether it's a conscious training approach taken by enlightened management, or simply the result of having been thrown into the deep end of the pool a few times, the learning becomes a reflex action, not something conscious or deliberate.

At the same time, the process does overwhelm people, and the results aren't pretty. While sometimes this failure results from the personality and temperament of a specific individual, a lot of times the failure results from a lack of overall support given by the organization.

It's vital that you watch for the signs of too much stress, and provide support when needed.

Managing Limbic Learning for Positive Results

How do you take charge of your limbic learning? The first step is to seek out challenging situations. Many people shy away from the sort of stress and challenge that would provide limbic learning opportunity, but the BKPM-in-the-making learns to welcome the challenge and the stress.

The situation alone doesn't make a BKPM, of course. The second step is to manage the overall stress and risk so that it pushes you to the edge, but not over it. That's a delicate balance, so the way to manage it is to put more weight on your side of the teeter-totter.

People who are cut off from human contact and relationships, or people who operate solo, often don't have the support structure that helps keep stress within limits. A BKPM needs a team. A BKPM-in-the-making needs a mentor — in fact, multiple mentors are better.

To achieve limbic learning, you must create a situation that imprints the right lessons on the mind of the learner. The Trane Company for many years operated "Project Management War Games," an intense around-the-clock four-day simulation of a project. Students were given a packet of information, developed a plan, sold the plan to "clients," managed "subcontractors," and dealt with an increasing set of problems and disasters as the imaginary project moved toward completion.

Students regularly reported that the training was one of the most powerful experiences of their lives, and many had the experience of finding themselves in stressful real-life situations that corresponded to the lessons they had already learned. The high stress of the training class was paired with the low risk that the project was imaginary, and no real failure was possible.

That's the key to building BKPMs in your organization: the combination of high stress and low risk. The high stress is easy enough, but the low risk requires some planning.

Interrogator Greg Hartley points out that US pilots and special forces personnel go through an imaginary POW experience known as SERE: Survival, Evasion, Resistance, and Escape. The military candidates go through an immensely high stakes process, with elements modeled on CIA psychological warfare practices. Stress is very high — as high as they can make it.

Unlike the real thing, however, students in the SERE program know it's a training class, know it will eventually end, and know that if it truly becomes too much, they can stop it. That makes the risk relatively low.

The combination of high stress and low risk enables people to internalize the lessons and be better prepared in the event of actual capture, and makes it easier for people to succeed and to internalize that feeling of success. Organized limbic learning can be a powerful tool.

Of course, real-life situations (high stress and high risk) create limbic learning as well. Unfortunately, real life can imprint the wrong lessons, or do enough damage to the trainee to eliminate the long-term value of the lesson. Be deliberate in your training approach and you'll get better — not to mention safer — results.

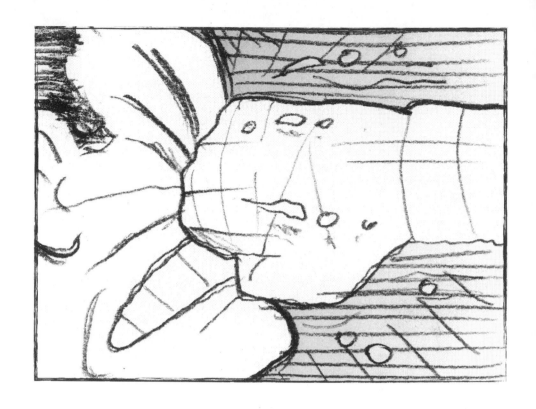

Conflict and
Communications

Managing Conflict

WHAT DO you think of when you think of conflict?

Common responses include anger, strong emotion, resentment, defensiveness, and argument — all of which can easily occur.

In its simplest form, however, "conflict" simply means disagreement. Disagreement is an everyday occurrence, and most disagreements get resolved easily and quickly. While strong negative emotion and bad reactions remain a danger, the BKPM must be fearless and direct to handle conflict before it gets out of hand.

Bruce Lee, as you'll recall, defined his *Jeet Kune Do* method as "the art of fighting without fighting." When it comes to conflict management and the BKPM, that's exactly the right approach to take. While it may not be feasible (or even desirable) to avoid every fight, most conflict situations can be resolved at a far more equitable and reasonable level.

In this chapter, we'll show you a model for understanding conflict, plotting your response to any conflict situation, and achieving the results you want from both a short-term and a long-term perspective.

Figure 7-1. The BKPM Conflict Resolution Model.
Different situations call for different modes of conflict resolution.

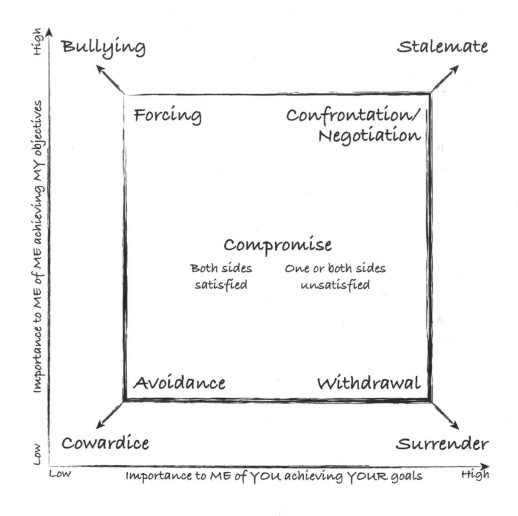

Methods of Conflict Management

Not every conflict situation should be approached in the same way. Sometimes the stakes are immediate and overwhelming; other times they are trivial and insignificant. Sometimes it's vital that your point of view carry the day — other times it's better if someone else wins.

That's why the first stage in conflict management is to select the right approach for the situation.

What is the right approach, and how do you determine what it is in a given situation? To answer that, we must first answer two questions:

1. How important is it to me to achieve my objectives in this conflict?
2. How important is it to me that you achieve your objectives in this conflict?

The first question is obvious. Do you have a dog in this fight? How important is it to you that you win or achieve your goal?

If your experience tells you that a certain technical choice on the project is going to cause trouble, it's important that you keep that choice from being made. If you're the leader and your leadership is being challenged, it may be important to make clear who's in charge. If the customer isn't going on the record about the project objective, you must make them do so.

The second question, however, is less obvious. This issue isn't whether the other person wants to achieve his or her objective, but whether you want them to.

There are a number of reasons why it might be important to you that the other person achieves his or her objective. First, that person might be the customer, and if the customer ain't happy, ain't nobody happy. Second, the other person may care more about the outcome than you do. If we're choosing where to go to lunch, you might not have a strong opinion, but if the other person has food restrictions, it's important that the restaurant serve appropriate food. Third, the long-term relationship may be more important than the short-term issue at stake. Winning today may set up a resentment that causes you to lose tomorrow.

To choose the correct conflict response, you need to know where you stand on both these issues. Figure 7-2 shows you how to make the right choice.

Figure 7-2. Choosing the Right Response. The best strategy for conflict management depends on your goals.

If...	My need to achieve my objective is...	My need for you to achieve your objective is...	Choose the conflict response...
	Low	Low	Avoidance
	Low	High	Withdrawal
	Medium	Medium	Compromise
	High	Low	Forcing
	High	High	Confrontation/ Negotiation

Avoidance

Imagine your extended family has gotten together for Thanksgiving. Sitting around the table, some cousin you haven't seen in years decides to bring up, say, the issue of abortion. No matter what position you hold on the issue, it's pretty clear that this conversation is headed for a bad end.

If your opinion and your imaginary cousin's opinion are diametrically opposed, it's very unlikely that a dinner-table argument is going to change anybody's mind. The most likely outcome is a ruined dinner for everybody.

What's the best strategy? Change the subject. Ignore the bait. Ask the imaginary cousin to bring up the topic at a more appropriate time. In other words, the conflict strategy most appropriate here is *avoidance*. You don't have to fight every battle, and you certainly don't have to fight on somebody else's timetable.

In a work environment, the same logic applies. Perhaps someone's raised a contentious side issue, but it's not important for the project at hand. Don't waste everybody's time — especially yours — on a conflict that really doesn't need to happen.

You may also use avoidance as a temporary tactic. If someone's lost his or her temper, the first order of business may be to get that person calmed down. Trying to work through substantive issues, no matter how important, when someone is consumed with emotion is usually doomed to failure. Deal with the emotional issue first, then adopt a new strategy to work through the problem.

If someone uses avoidance to run away from an issue that should be confronted, that's a different strategy. That's *cowardice*, and it's a bad idea. Avoiding unnecessary conflict is smart; avoiding important conflict will sooner or later do harm to the project — and to you.

Withdrawal

Earlier, we mentioned a conflict about where to have lunch. That's (usually) trivial, but it still qualifies as conflict: it's a disagreement. If you really don't have a strong opinion in the matter, you may choose to resolve the conflict by yielding to the other person's wishes in the matter. That's called *withdrawal*.

When problem-solver and BKPM Winston Wolf starts giving orders to the two hit men in *Pulp Fiction*, one of them (John Travolta's character, Vincent) balks. "A 'please' would be nice," he says.

Wolf's immediate response is annoyance, but he decides to explain himself instead. "If I'm curt with you, it's because time is a factor. I think fast, I talk fast, and I need you guys to act fast…. So pretty please, with sugar on top, clean the [expletive deleted] car."

Wolf's agenda is to get this situation resolved quickly and well. A conflict with Vincent over something as simple as "please" won't address anybody's real need. The "please" matters to Vincent, and saying "please" (or "pretty please with sugar on top") costs Wolf little or nothing.

Standing on principle on every little issue adds dramatically to the supply of stress and unhappiness in your life, and accomplishes very little. Giving in on the small stuff lets you reserve your attention for the issues that matter.

There's a secondary benefit to withdrawal as a conflict management technique. Psychologist Robert Cialdini describes the "Rule of Reciprocity," the internal pressure that pushes us to repay in kind whatever another person has provided us. (Cialdini, 17).

That's not simply a commitment to the Golden Rule. Cialdini argues that the rule is so deeply ingrained in human nature that it tends to work no matter what the circumstances. If you give in on an issue, even if it's a small one — even if the other person doesn't actually care about it very much — you dramatically increase the likelihood that the other person will tend to reciprocate, and give in on another issue — potentially one that matters to you much more.

When you yield to the other person's wishes not out of choice but rather because you think you're going to lose the conflict, withdrawal turns into *surrender*. Sometimes you're certain to be defeated, so surrender may make sense as a strategy in certain cases. As long as there's hope of victory, however, it may make greater sense to fight on. Other tactics — compromise and negotiation — may help you eke out at least a partial victory.

Compromise

As that great negotiator Mick Jagger sang, "You can't always get what you want/But if you try real hard, you might just get what you need." If your needs and the needs of the other party are less than total, a *compromise* may resolve the issue satisfactorily.

In a compromise, you settle for less than your ultimate goal, and so does the other person. If you propose a price of $1 million and the other side counters with $500,000, you might agree on $750,000. Whether that's a good deal or not depends on your costs. If it's going to cost you $800,000 to fulfill the contract, then meeting the other side half way isn't an acceptable option. You're still going to lose money.

The important consideration in a compromise is whether both parties feel that they have gotten an acceptable outcome. If we're arguing with our spouse about whether to vacation on the beach or in the mountains, and we decide to compromise and vacation in the city, we may have swapped one unhappy person for two unhappy people. That's not an improvement.

Compromise is also not simply about splitting the difference. A traditional bargaining technique is to make your initial offer far below what you're willing to pay (or far above what you're willing to accept), because splitting the difference will actually move the final price dramatically in your direction. Watch out for bargainers who try to tilt the field prematurely.

Forcing

"It's my way or the highway." There are times and situations where you don't really care (or can't afford to care) what other people think or want — it's necessary that you impose your will on the situation and move forward. That's *forcing*, and sometimes you have to do it.

The disadvantages with forcing are obvious. First, you're likely to encounter resistance. Second, you can't easily force someone who has more power than you do. Third, even when you win, you may create long-term hostility that can complicate a later situation.

While good leadership and good judgment will help you identify times and places where forcing is the right strategic choice, there are several situations that call immediately for forcing:

- **When you have no time.** Often, you can achieve the same results with negotiation that you can with forcing, but negotiation takes time. When a decision or action must take place immediately, debate may not be an option.

- **When other strategies fail.** You may be perfectly willing to negotiate or even compromise, but if the other party is unwilling or unable to move, forcing is often the only option available to you.

- **When a choice has to be made.** It may be that more than one choice is legitimate and defensible, but a choice still has to be made. In such situations, it's often the job of the leader to make the call and to force a common direction on the entire team or project.

When leaders rely on forcing as a favorite style, ignoring opportunities for empowerment, team involvement, and participation, forcing all too easily turns into *bullying*.

Confrontation/Negotiation

Harvard Negotiation Project researchers Roger Fisher and William Ury tell the story of the two sisters fighting over the last orange. They agree to compromise, cutting the orange in half. The first sister takes her half, eats the fruit, and throws away the peel. The other sister throws away the fruit, and takes the peel into the kitchen to use in the cake she is baking. (Fisher and Ury, 59)

Negotiation differs from compromise because it seeks a "win/win" outcome rather than splitting the difference. It's possible because the issues in a conflict aren't always reciprocal (*e.g.*, my victory requires your loss), but can often be resolved in a way that allows both parties to get all (or at least most) of what they want and need.

Negotiators have to confront the conflict directly, look for the root cause, identify the underlying goals and objectives of each party, build mutual trust, and find a solution to achieve the "win/win" objective. Skill in negotiation is one of the most important things a BKPM can bring to the table, especially when navigating the complex relationships of the three-sided table.

Given a choice between studying project management techniques and studying negotiation, we think a BKPM is better off in the long run by sharpening and improving negotiation skills.

Some authorities, including PMI®, use the term *confrontation* instead of negotiation when describing the different approaches to conflict resolution. PMI® training materials, in fact, often claim that confrontation is the most important and effective method of dealing with conflict, but that assumes a "one size fits all" view of conflict that we think is simplistic and wrong-headed.

There is no one single correct approach to conflict, as we've seen. Effective BKPMs switch easily back and forth among the different styles of conflict resolution based on what's most appropriate for the situation at hand.

There are potential problems and limitations in negotiation. First, negotiation usually takes time and effort, and not all issues are worth the necessary investment.

Second, not every issue contains a win/win opportunity. However, many more issues do have a win/win option than you'd think — but you often have to look for it.

Third, and perhaps most importantly, effective negotiation requires that the parties have some degree of mutual trust. When you look at trouble spots around the globe, what stands in the way of a solution isn't so much finding a win/win, but rather establishing enough trust to make a deal possible in the first place.

When negotiation fails, for whatever reason, the result is *stalemate*. The BKPM must then take a different approach to resolve the conflict.

Planning for Conflict

We've emphasized that an effective BKPM is an "honest broker" in the relationship between the customer and the implementation team. Both sides necessarily depend on the BKPM's objectivity, honesty, and clarity whenever difficult issues and conflicts arise.

One important part of any conflict management strategy is how people view you, and that's something that can only be developed over the long haul. Such qualities as being genuine and generous, having a customer perspective, and practicing transparency provide numerous benefits.

Your empathy — your ability to recognize and acknowledge the emotions and issues of the other person, whether or not you agree with them — brings people closer. In conflict resolution, they're all important assets. Cultivate them over the long haul, and you'll find almost every conflict situation works out better.

The Role of Trust

To depend on a BKPM's objectivity, honesty, and clarity requires *trust*. By the time a conflict occurs, it's too late to start building trust. Conflict — especially mismanaged conflict — tends to erode trust, and once gone, it's hard to replace. That trust relationship is especially critical when the ship is out at sea, half way through the journey, and being battered by storms, mutinies, and scurvy.

There are at least three important types of trust in the BKPM/Owner/Team relationship. The first is the trust that comes from integrity and honesty: *character-based trust*. If someone tells the truth 90 percent of the time and lies 10 percent of the time, we call that person a liar. Even a small lapse in character can loom large in someone's decision whether to trust you. A BKPM must always keep his or her word. Only make promises you intend to keep.

A second type of trust is *competency-based trust*. You can have a lot of integrity and still be completely incompetent — but that doesn't create meaningful trust. At the beginning of the project, when people don't yet know you, the evidence of your competency is your existing track record. As you get into the project, your track record becomes irrelevant: your competency is assessed based on today's project results.

A third type of trust is *prediction-based trust*. The BKPM essentially promises to achieve an agreed-upon outcome, which involves making certain predictions as to how a given strategy or approach will work. BKPMs make predictions about potential risks and the effect of risk mitigation strategies. BKPMs interpret the tea leaves of the external environment, to prepare for the inevitable environmental changes that can sweep away previously established project assumptions.

Physicist Niels Bohr famously said, "Prediction is very difficult, especially about the future." (This is also often attributed to Yogi Berra.) However, BKPMs are frequently held accountable for making predictions no matter how uncertain the environment. And more importantly, sometimes the honesty required can be brutal. The BKPM can't shy away from the necessity, but you can provide empathy in the process.

The way we can do this is to go back to one of the core principles of project management: *Preparation is cheaper than problem solving.*

Conflict is not only inevitable in projects; it's usually predictable as well. Risk and uncertainty is baked in. The BKPM can usually anticipate most areas of potential project stress and, better yet, prepare for them.

That's one of the most important reasons for effective risk management, as we discussed in Chapter Four.

Situation → Behavior → Outcome

People are usually predisposed to particular conflict management styles. Some people avoid conflict reflexively. Others are ready to go to DEFCON One at the slightest hint of trouble. Modifying these natural tendencies is an awareness of the dynamics of a particular situation. If your spouse criticizes your driving, you're probably going to react differently than if a police officer does.

The difficulty is that these decisions are often made on a very short timeline, resulting in failure to understand the dynamics and ramifications of the situation. Coupled with the natural tendency to react in a certain way, we end up with the driver yelling at the police officer — not a winning strategy in most circumstances.

The three-step process for avoiding emotion-driven reactive behavior is known as SBO: Situation, Behavior, and Outcome. In the SBO model, you describe a situation, identify the relevant behaviors, and show how they relate to the outcome.

That works well when you're telling a story about a past situation, but it doesn't quite tell you how to plan for a current or future one. When you're looking at a potential problem or conflict trigger on your project, you need to first identify the situation that promises trouble, and second to define the outcome you would like. Then — and only then —

are you in a position to strategize the specific behaviors and actions necessary to link situation to outcome.

Owner Pressures

In the three-sided table, we define the customer as the "outcome owner," and that role creates important, and often unspoken, pressures. The person directly identified as the customer may not actually be the end customer, but rather is an intermediary. If the corporate CEO wants a new data system, the CIO gets the job. The CIO, in turn, may appoint a senior staffer to be the "customer" from the point of view of the project manager and of the team. The BKPM sometimes has access to these higher-level customers, but often does not.

Even if the official customer *is* the real customer, he or she may not be the only one. Projects often have constituencies, and within the project's constituency, there may be multiple (and sometimes incompatible) needs and objectives. These external project stakeholders may have significant political power, and this makes the outcome owner subject to a wide range of pressures.

The BKPM's role is not merely to broker the relationship between outcome owner and implementation team, but also to "have the back" of the front-line customer. In other words, the BKPM acts as COO to the customer's CEO, and in turn acts as the CEO to the project team.

The BKPM must be aware, sympathetic, and supportive of the front-line customer. This makes conflict between the BKPM and outcome owner even more sensitive. The front-line customer has to believe that the BKPM will act to protect the customer, and anything that undermines that essential trust can be devastating to the project.

Access Portals

The BKPM must build *access portals* — and sometimes *escape portals* — into the project plan to bridge the gap with the customer when conflicts and problems arise. This goes back to our earlier understanding that the best strategy for conflict management and resolution is to be prepared for it well in advance of the actual need.

Access (and escape) portals come into being as a result of understanding the project context and preparing for risks, as shown in Figure 7-3.

Here's an example of how access portals work.

In our discussion of the Triple Constraint, we identified that there was by definition some flexibility in the Weak Constraint. When you as a BKPM help the customer understand the project dynamic, you both reach an advance agreement as to what sort of slippage is acceptable, and what is not.

When a situation arises that upsets the original course of the project, the BKPM steers the damage into the Weak Constraint, where it will do least harm. Because the BKPM has *already* reached an understanding with the customer, there isn't any conflict. It's been dealt with in advance.

Figure 7-3. Access Portals. The BKPM must build "access portals" into the project to bridge the gap with the customer when conflicts and problems arise.

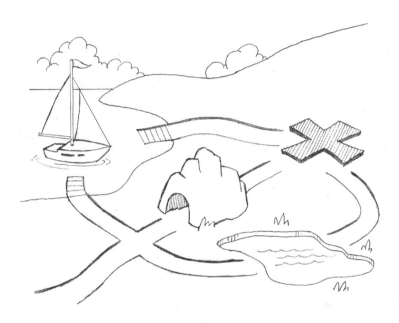

A good project manager identifies critical risks that can affect the project objective and creates plans and strategies to deal with them if they occur. Of course, we all prefer that risks just pass us by, but in the real world, that's not always the case. Because the BKPM reviews risks and responses with the customer in advance, when a risk actually occurs, there's already advance agreement on how we will respond.

Another type of escape portal is created when the BKPM is transparent on the use of resources, both in the plan and in the project execution. No matter how much effort or skill is applied, sometimes the project begins to consume more than was planned. Rather than let the situation fester, the BKPM works with the customer to diagnose the problem, and supports the customer in the executive decision to continue the project — or cancel it before things get out of hand.

Customers are often in a delicate position. They may not always have the technical understanding, nor experience in the kinds of issues that often arise. In the customer/BKPM relationship, the BKPM has P&L responsibility for the project, but the customer owns the cost/benefit analysis. You provide information on how much it will cost, but only the customer can decide if it's worth it.

Access portals and escape portals aren't ways for a BKPM to dodge operational responsibility for the project, but rather are ways to enhance it. When a BKPM is prepared for trouble, and the strategies are laid down and shared in advance, conflict is avoided and the BKPM and customer can push forward on the same page.

The Kranz
Dictum

Plan for Trouble Long Before It Arrives

On January 21, 1967, during a launch pad test of what was intended to be the first manned mission of the Apollo program, a cabin fire broke out. Astronauts Gus Grissom, Edward White, and Roger Chaffee perished in that fire.

The accident review board was never able to pinpoint the exact cause of the fire, but what they found was worse: a series of design and construction flaws that made catastrophe all too likely. When the Apollo 1 capsule was shipped to Kennedy Space Center, there were 113 significant incomplete planned engineering changes. After delivery, NASA issued an astounding additional 623 engineering change orders!

Gus Grissom was reportedly so upset that he hung a lemon on the simulator. After expressing their concerns about the amount of flammable material in the cabin, the astronauts gave the program manager, Joseph Shea, a portrait of the three astronauts praying, with a caption that read, "It isn't that we don't trust you, Joe, but this time we've decided to go over your head." (Figure 8-1)

Alas, the appeal to higher authority was not successful.

Figure 8-1. Apollo 1 Parody Crew Portrait. Concerned with engineering issues on the Apollo 1 spacecraft, astronauts Gus Grissom, Edward White, and Roger Chaffee created this crew portrait for program manager Joseph Shea, captioned, "It isn't that we don't trust you, Joe, but this time we've decided to go over your head."

From left to right, Edward White, Gus Grissom, and Roger Chaffee

Of course, no project, no matter how well run, can be immune to all disasters, and the BKPM is never so presumptuous as to think he or she can control all risk. While any particular accident can usually be avoided, it's absurd to think they *all* can be.

Grissom himself recognized the unavoidable risks in spaceflight. "You sort of have to put that out of your mind," he said in a 1966 interview. "There's always a possibility that you can have a catastrophic failure, of course; this can happen on any flight; it can happen on the last one as well as the first one. So, you just plan as best you can to take care of all these eventualities, and you get a well-trained crew and you go fly."

The key words in Grissom's statement are *plan* and *well-trained*. The BKPM knows that problems and mistakes are inevitable, and *designs the process with that in mind*.

While there wasn't anything NASA could do about Apollo 1, there was a lot they could do about future Apollo missions. In fact, one of the key reasons Apollo 13 returned safely to Earth has to do with the reaction to Apollo 1. Mission director and BKPM Gene Kranz developed the "Kranz Dictum," which guided the response. When the next failure inevitably happened, the team was prepared. Plans had been laid in, and everyone was well trained.

The Kranz Dictum needs to be part of every BKPM's toolkit.

The Kranz Dictum

One of the big reasons that the Apollo 13 crew returned safely to Earth is because of the actions of NASA lead flight director (and BKPM) Gene Kranz.

In the movie version of *Apollo 13*, Kranz (played by Ed Harris) frequently says, "Failure is not an option!" The quote is made up for the movie, but the sentiment is real.

Here's the real story.

Figure 8-2. Apollo 13 Mission Control. Mission Control celebrates splashdown of Apollo 13. Gene Kranz is second from the left, clapping.

Following the launchpad fire of Apollo 1, which killed astronauts Gus Grissom, Ed White, and Roger Chaffee, Gene Kranz spoke to his team the following Monday and delivered what became known as the "Kranz Dictum."

Here's what he said.

Spaceflight will never tolerate carelessness, incapacity, and neglect. Somewhere, somehow, we screwed up. It could have been in design, build, or test. Whatever it was, we should have caught it.

We were too gung ho about the schedule and we locked out all of the problems we saw each day in our work. Every element of the program was in trouble and so were we. The simulators were not working, Mission Control was behind in virtually every area, and the flight and test procedures changed daily. Nothing we did had any shelf life. Not one of us stood up and said, "Dammit, stop!"

I don't know what Thompson's committee [investigating the accident] will find as the cause, but I know what I find. We are the cause! We were not ready! We did not do our job. We were rolling the dice, hoping that things would come together by launch day, when in our hearts we knew it would take a miracle. We were pushing the schedule and betting that the Cape would slip before we did.

From this day forward, Flight Control will be known by two words: "Tough and Competent." *Tough* means we are forever accountable for what we do or what we fail to do. We will never again compromise our responsibilities. Every time we walk into Mission Control we will know what we stand for.

Competent means we will never take anything for granted. We will never be found short in our knowledge and in our skills. Mission Control will be perfect.

When you leave this meeting today you will go to your office and the first thing you will do there is to write "Tough and Competent" on your blackboards. It will never be erased. Each day when you enter the room these words will remind you of the price paid by Grissom, White, and Chaffee. These words are the price of admission to the ranks of Mission Control." (Wasser, 2005)

Face the Future, Not the Past

The traditional project manager isn't part of the three-sided table; he or she is part of the project team. Accountable for the team process but not accountable for the project vision or objective, the traditional project manager does what he or she is told. Since vision issues are at the heart of most project failures, this yields a mixture of successful and unsuccessful outcomes — *no matter how good the traditional project manager is!*

When a BKPM enters the picture, the roles shift. The BKPM is accountable for the vision process. If a project is wrong or unrealistic, the BKPM confronts the issue before the project even gets started, using forced clarification as a process to bring the project in line with reality. Either the vision (performance criteria/scope) changes, the circumstances (resources/time) change, or the project needs to be rethought — sometimes even cancelled.

As we've noted, the BKPM doesn't create the vision, but is still responsible for the process that establishes it. The BKPM pushes back against both customer and team, and oversees course corrections as the project unfolds.

Visions are necessarily rooted in reality. You can't just imagine some castle in the sky and call it a project vision — though sadly, it happens all the time. A real vision starts with a clear understanding of the current situation and a realistic appraisal of the available resources and constraints that shape its accomplishment. The outcome of the project can be a stretch goal, but it can't be detached from the art of the possible.

When a project is in trouble, it's necessary to revisit the vision. If reality — constraints, needs, resources, and issues — has shifted, the objective may shift as well. Moving the goal posts is sometimes legitimate — and sometimes necessary. Sometimes the goal posts move on their own, whether you want them to or not.

Sometimes, a project needs to be terminated before it spirals out of control. Other times, we learn that the customer needs have evolved, and the project as originally specified no long solves the underlying problem. Things have to change. Although nobody enjoys hearing bad news, the BKPM has to step up to the plate early.

A change in vision isn't the same thing as a failure of the project. Apollo 1 was an unambiguous failure, but Apollo 13 was not. Apollo 13's original objective was to go to the Moon, but when one of the oxygen tanks exploded, the vision and mission changed. The old goal was no longer operative, and a new goal — get the astronauts home safely — took center stage.

When the Project Has Already Failed

Sometimes failure isn't the end of the project, but rather the beginning. In other words, as in the case of Apollo 13, we undertake some projects because disaster has already occurred.

Sometimes, the disaster is outside the project. If a hurricane hits the data center, it's not a failure on the part of data center management. If the data center construction didn't take extreme weather into account, however, that *does* constitute a failure of management of a different project.

Other times, the disaster is inside the project. If building the data center is six months behind schedule and $2 million over budget, there's probably something wrong with the vision, performance, or environment.

In both cases, the recovery and rescue effort is a *separate* project. If you're called in because the data center is late and over budget, you start with where you are: late and over budget.

Measuring success under these circumstances is relative. If you're already past the deadline to open the new data center, you can't very well get the center opened on time —

not unless you have a time machine, anyway. And that $2 million is already spent; you can't get it back. The question isn't how well you can perform against the original baseline, but how well and quickly you can get the job done from whenever you're forced to start.

Be Honest and Thorough About Project Risks

No project manager — not even the BKPM — has a crystal ball. Rumsfeld's famous "unknown unknowns" lurk in the darkness, waiting to trip you up. Good risk management helps a lot. Actively search for the kinds of risks and issues likely to harm your project. Adjust the project plan to protect yourself when you can; keep some reserves and flexibility to deal with the rest. Share your knowledge with other stakeholders. The project vision has to include consideration of risks, or it's incomplete.

What about the unknown unknowns? Isn't it true that no matter how good you are, sometimes things just happen? Well, yes…but that doesn't mean you can't be ready for it. Earlier we listed a number of strategies for managing unknown unknowns. Notice they all require getting out in front of the problem.

We use the term "acts of God" because some of the things we do as humans have risks that can only be controlled by God Himself. That is not, however, an excuse for disregarding or ignoring them. Many risk management plans deal only with manageable risks, but that gives you an unrealistic picture of your project situation.

Was the loss of the Apollo 1 astronauts preventable? With 20-20 hindsight, the answer is clearly yes. Project pressures, especially in the time constraint, combined with the complexity and newness of the technology, increased the risk of something going wrong. Given the inherent tension, there's tremendous pressure on project managers to push forward and hope for the best.

From our BKPM perspective, this constitutes a failure of the three-sided table. In the case of Apollo 1, the Apollo Spacecraft Program Office Manager was responsible for managing the design and construction of both command module and lunar module — but his mandate was to run the technical side of the shop, not to serve as the independent broker between owner and solutions team. As a result, he didn't have the positional authority to call a halt when the sheer number of engineering changes threatened to overwhelm the project.

While Gene Kranz managed to become a BKPM within the NASA environment, the design of the organization didn't encourage or support that kind of initiative, and he succeeded through grit and determination. A strong leader, he was willing to push back against management as well as to demand excellence from the team.

By the time of the *Challenger* disaster, the three-sided table had collapsed once again. One of the members of the accident investigation commission was well-known physicist Richard

Feynman. Rather than stick to the investigation channels established by the commission leadership, Feynman talked to frontline managers and technical personnel. "When I left the meeting [with NASA engineers]," he wrote, "I had the definite impression that I had found the same game as with the [O-ring] seals: management reducing criteria and accepting more and more errors that weren't designed into the device, while the engineers are screaming from below, 'HELP!' and 'This is a RED ALERT!'" (Dobson and Feickert, 23)

The danger in the two-sided table is made very clear by the fact that NASA management put the risk of catastrophic shuttle failure at about 100,000 to 1, while the engineering consensus was that it was closer to 300 to 1. Considering the actual track record of shuttle flights, the real number appears to be about 50 to 1.

Clearly, however, there was no one in the loop to bridge the gap between the two assessments of risk. The lack of a functioning BKPM was a proximate cause of the disaster.

It is inevitable that people, over time, lower their guard as a reaction to the insidiousness of chance and probability. When people live with risks that never happen, they start to forget that the risk even exists — then, *SMACK!* the risk happens.

The Kranz Dictum should remind us that risk never goes away.

Don't Hide Bad News

In a project with the UK Ministry of Defense involving high-stakes testing for senior managers, past problems with the process had led to mandated governmental oversight and monitoring to ensure consistency and fairness in the project.

Unfortunately, a BKPM was *not* at the helm. There were serious underlying problems. Personnel were constantly changing. Long days were common. Software tools were obsolete. Only heroic action on the part of team members kept the project from collapsing on the spot.

The project manager, however, did not share these problems with the customer. When asked, he repeated told everyone that things were fine, but he was holding the project together with sheer force and a good dose of luck.

Then it came time to renew the project.

In a competitive bid situation with a great deal of cost pressure, the project manager's failure to raise the alarm early meant that the company couldn't suddenly add in a huge amount of money to upgrade. Had the project manager been forthright about the problems all along, the bid could have included an upgrade requirement, and those problems could have been dealt with. Both the project manager and her employer were left vulnerable.

There's an old *Saturday Night Live* skit where a Russian news reporter in Chernobyl is saying, "Nothing is wrong here. Especially near the nuclear reactor." It's better to say it now than to wait until disaster is upon us.

The effective BKPM will never wait until the last minute to face the truth, no matter how unpleasant it may be. Often, the problem can be solved, albeit at a cost. In some cases it may be necessary to walk away from the project altogether, or at least to dramatically rethink the whole thing. In both cases, the problem usually gets worse the longer you wait.

The question of *how* you present bad news is also important. Again, preparation is the best tool you have going for you. Figure 8-3 provides additional tools to present bad news or problem issues in the most effective manner possible.

Figure 8-3. Tools for Presenting Bad News. The need to deliver bad news may happen to any project manager. Prepare in advance by using the following strategies.

- Don't own the outcome; own the process

- Problem-solve the solution. Come up with multiple approaches. The old saw, "Don't bring me problems, bring me answers" is good policy, even though it's not always possible.

- Don't commit to one solution alone, but rather develop a set of options to present to the customer so you can make the decision jointly. This is true even if there's only one good option. Add some less-good options into the mix because lots of people want to feel there's a choice, no matter how constrained.

- Avoid being maneuvered into a solution prematurely. The "ready-fire-aim" syndrome has sunk many projects. An answer that makes the situation worse is always possible, so make sure to "murder board" your solutions.

- Cultivate your "walk away" power. If you're seen as someone out to protect his or her own role at all costs, no one will see you as an honest broker. When you put the project ahead of your own career interest, the gain in extra trust actually increases the likelihood of your survival.

Embrace Redundancy and a Certain Amount of Inefficiency

It may sound strange for a BKPM to embrace redundancy and a certain amount of inefficiency, but both of these are invaluable tools for managing a troubled project. For example, part of the survival of Apollo 13 was because someone put together an emergency kit that contained duct tape. No duct tape, no improvised CO_2 filters.

Of course, that same emergency kit was also on every other Apollo flight — and generally went unused. That's inefficiency in action. Most spacecraft systems contain redundancy. If one fails, the mission doesn't end in catastrophe because the backup is there to take up the slack.

It's reasonable to debate how much redundancy and how much inefficiency is appropriate to the level of actual project risk, but as long as risk and uncertainty are part of your project environment, build in some margin to help you manage it.

Redundancy and a certain amount of inefficiency can be highly desirable when you're managing projects with significant risk. Things *will* go wrong, and having some flexibility in the project parameters to deal with them dramatically increases your odds of success. Think about the kinds of resources you'll need to cope with the unexpected. By the time you experience the emergency, it's too late to put together the kit.

Training and preparation are part of the inefficiency and redundancy in a project. We train people for work above and beyond their daily responsibilities; we prepare for eventualities that never happen. We said earlier that part of becoming a BKPM is having enough real world experience (which usually includes the bruises and scars to show for it). But a capable BKPM isn't enough without a trained and ready team to do the work. Preparing an organization for crisis response takes effort and time. Expend the effort and time all along so you have the capability ready when you need it.

Use the Eisenhower Grid to Prioritize Efforts

General and President Dwight D. Eisenhower (another BKPM) said, "What is important is seldom urgent, and what is urgent is seldom important." He grouped his action items into four quadrants, illustrated in Figure 8-4.

Figure 8-4. The Eisenhower Grid. Sort action items into four quadrants to set proper priorities.

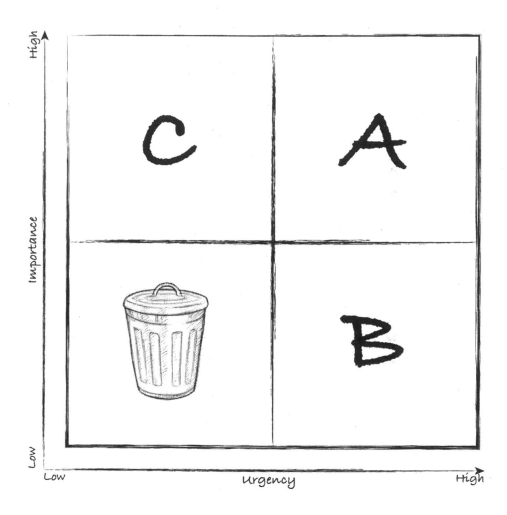

- **Group A** is reserved for tasks that are both *important* and *urgent* — a textbook description of a *crisis*. Those tasks get done immediately and personally. That doesn't necessarily mean that you do every aspect of them yourself, but that you oversee the work directly and are accountable for it personally.

- **Group B** tasks are those that are *urgent*, but *not important*. They get delegated, both the work and the oversight. A lot of *busywork* falls into Group B.

- **Group C** tasks are *important*, but *not urgent.* While they have long-term benefit, the lack of urgency means they often fall through the cracks. Setting an end date gives those tasks a bit of artificial urgency and increases the likelihood they get done. Those also get overseen personally. Group C tasks, by definition, are *proactive*.

- The **Trashcan** contains tasks that are *neither important nor urgent*. They're *trivial*, and can be dropped altogether (or at least delegated to somebody else). If a job's not worth doing in the first place, don't do it poorly — just don't do it.

While crisis management (Group A) is clearly necessary, notice that all the things you do to get ready for a crisis, such as training, always fall into Group B. They're important — critically important — but because they aren't urgent, we often don't get around to doing them at all.

Manage Both Facts and Feelings

If there has to be conflict between BKPM and outcome owner, try to have it in the vision phase (or in the case of a troubled project, the modification of vision phase). Can the project be accomplished in a satisfactory manner within the available resources and time? If the answer is no, it doesn't do the customer any favors to go ahead. Don't reenact the Charge of the Light Brigade on somebody else's dime.

If you have an unreasonable project owner who demands the project move forward, remember that if you accept the project, you become accountable for delivering. Don't set yourself up for unnecessary and inappropriate failure.

When Winston Wolf arrives at the scene of the problem in *Pulp Fiction*, transparency and situational awareness are uppermost in his mind. "About the car," he asks. "Is there anything I need to know? Does it stall, does it make a lot of noise, does it smoke, is there gas in it, anything?" If the car has problems, he will either have to modify his strategy or abort the project.

Fortunately, Vincent answers him by saying, "Aside from how it looks, the car's cool."

But the BKPM can't afford to take empty assurance for granted. "Positive?" Wolf asks. "Don't get me out on the road and I find out the brake lights don't work."

It's only when Wolf is satisfied that the circumstances of the project are as represented that he's willing to move forward. When you own responsibility for the project's process, you must know all the relevant facts.

Watch out for emotion. Under stress, it's all too easy to get caught up in the emotional "fight or flight" syndrome, when the limbic system kicks in and complicates your thinking process. Smooth the potential conflict by positioning the three-sided table toward problem solving rather than blamestorming. Figure 8-5 provides some useful phrases.

Figure 8-5. Problem-Solving Phrasebook. Prepare in advance so that in the event of problems, you can say the following:

- "We said there were risks, and we discussed this risk."
- "We agreed that if this risk occurred, we would take the following actions."
- "We need to regroup and evaluate this new situation before moving forward."
- "Let's discuss possible reactions and determine our next steps."
- "Based on these developments, let's determine the new outcome that will best satisfy your needs."

Advance preparation is key. Your objective must be to handle the new circumstance or risk event calmly, as if it had been a possible outcome all the time.

Change the dynamic. Change the perspective. If there's opposition, look at the problem from the opponent's point of view. Help the project owner clarify the vision. Work to develop mutual options.

The Next Bout

The Program and the Project

W HEN JOHN L. SULLIVAN, Muhammad Ali, or Bruce Lee
finishes a fight, it's time to get ready for the next bout. A
fighter's career consists of many encounters. A champion
fighter manages his career as effectively as he manages each
individual bout.

As we know, the fundamental characteristic of a project is
that it ends. That's what distinguishes it from operational
(everyday) work. The BKPM, on the other hand, goes on. A
BKPM may be something more than just a project manager:
he or she might be a senior manager or executive with
ongoing responsibilities. Other times, a BKPM moves from
project to project, and in the overlap often becomes
responsible for more than a single project.

The transition from project to project, or between projects
and on-going work, has special issues as well. A BKPM
understands how to bridge the different roles and what steps
are needed to move from one bout to the next.

If the organization delivers projects to customers (in other
words, the BKPM is customer-facing), the BKPM is also part
of the sales and marketing team. BKPMs identify potential
areas for new business, provide technical understanding and
insight to account managers to help them sell new business,
and support the overall sales effort for new work.

And, of course, the BKPM provides a competitive
advantage. What makes one contractor better than another?

One key consideration is always the quality of its leadership. A BKPM, by his or her very nature, is viewed by customers as a senior executive; their track record of execution earns them that position. With a BKPM on your team, your case for winning the business gets much stronger. Who wouldn't want Gene Krantz on their space mission, Fred Astaire in their musical, or Winston Wolf cleaning up their mess? BKPMs not only get the job done, they get the job.

Closing Time (Come Back Tomorrow)

One oddity you'll find in many project plans, including plans developed by supposed project management experts, is that they often stop dead when the technical work ends. They leave out the often complex and sometimes dangerous process of closing out the project and transferring the results to their new owners. There's often a lot more work here than you'd think.

Once the project is (a) complete, (b) turned over, and (c) closed out internally, there are two additional steps you must do — not so much because they benefit the current project (that's over now), but because they set you up for the next bout.

As we've said, BKPMs need experience and the accompanying wisdom that goes along with it. Here's how to make that a systematic process, not only for you, but also for any future BKPMs that may be part of this project.

The two steps are (a) measurement of the outcome, and (b) lessons learned through the process.

Measurement of the Outcome

It's at the end of the project that you learn again how vital it is to define the objective at the beginning. There's an old management joke: The customer says, "Bring me a rock."

The project manager gets a rock and brings it back to the customer. "No," the customer says, "that's not the rock I wanted."

The project manager goes and gets a different rock. "No, that's not it either." And so on.

Unless you define the nature (and often the reason) of the rock you want, the project's in deep trouble even before you start work. If the definition of project success comes down to personal opinion, customers trump BKPMs or team members, and higher rank beats lower rank. In some cases, there isn't any other legitimate way to measure success, so we fall back on the traditional principle, "If mama ain't happy, ain't nobody happy."

Fortunately, that happens in the minority of projects. In most cases, you can measure the degree of success using objective criteria. The best way to do that, of course, is to establish those criteria at the outset.

Traditionally, objectives must be S-M-A-R-T, or sometimes S-M-A-R-T-E-R. These criteria help define and measure whether you have a properly stated and framed goal in place.

Figure 9-1. S-M-A-R-T and S-M-A-R-T-E-R. Your project objective must satisfy these conditions in order to make the project possible.

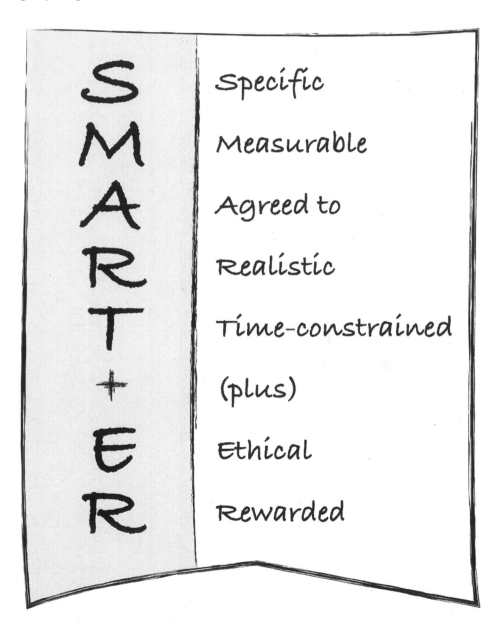

Whether you prefer "S-M-A-R-T" or decide you prefer being "S-M-A-R-T-E-R," make sure that your objective meets one additional criterion: able to be measured at *interim milestones*. It's a dangerous idea to wait until the end of the project before you can tell whether you made the goal or not. Being able to check progress at key intervals gives you the opportunity to make course corrections before it's too late.

If you can't measure it, it isn't real — and it's hard to get paid for it. Beginning with the three-sided table approach to developing the goal, process, and methodology, the BKPM approach emphasizes the importance of concrete, realistic goals. Those goals are always and necessarily measurable. Identifying the appropriate measurement of the outcome is inherently linked to the goal itself.

What if the nature of the project changes? As we discussed in the previous chapter, it's always possible for problems, evolving needs, and environmental factors to force a change in the project, and that means old goals and old metrics can become overtaken by events. The BKPM solution is to evolve the metrics along simultaneously with the objectives. This must be done at the same time, negotiating within the project's triple constraints. Synchronizing goals and metrics post-mortem doesn't work.

Don't Do "Lessons Learned"

Every book on project management agrees on the importance of a "lessons learned" activity at the end of the project.

We disagree. "Lessons learned" in real life almost always turn out to be completely useless. Figure 9-2 gives some reasons why.

Figure 9-2. Why "Lessons Learned" Aren't Useful.
Although "lessons learned" make sense in theory, in practice they are a lot less useful than you'd think.

1. The pressure of new work makes us skip them.

2. Most people and organizations never learn how to do them right.

3. "Lessons learned" too often turns into "blamestorming," in which the goal is figuring out who to pin it on rather than how to make it better.

4. Even when lessons learned are done well, the recommendations sit on the shelf and don't get used to improve future projects.

Recovering Value

Instead of futile "lessons learned" project post-mortems, in BKPM we use a more powerful technique: *recovering project value.*

As we've discussed, part of becoming a BKPM is acquiring the wisdom from your experience. That's usually the argument for you to do "lessons learned" on an almost continual basis, whether you're supported by the rest of your organization (and team) or not. But if it doesn't work — and it doesn't — you need something else instead.

Post-it® Notes, that essential tool of project management, was an incidental byproduct of a failed project. A 3M scientist accidentally developed a "low tack" adhesive, but nobody could figure out what it was good for until a colleague used it to stick a bookmark in his hymnal.

You do a lot of creative work on a project, and the act of facing and solving problems may open up doors that no one expected. Ask yourself and your team what secondary benefits may be extracted from the project, and you may be pleasantly rewarded.

Operational experience translates into better projects. As General (and BKPM) Ulysses S. Grant said, "It is well and wise to learn from our mistakes, but I prefer to learn from the mistakes of others."

What distinguishes a BKPM "recovering value" process from "lessons learned" is that the BKPM approach focuses on the future, not the past. It avoids "blamestorming." It looks at much more than just the plan and the process. It insists on follow-through. We want to know not merely what the lessons are, but how exactly we plan to implement those lessons for future projects.

In other words, "recovering value" isn't the last task of the old project. It's the *first* task of the *next* project.

Individual Incentives vs. Organizational Incentives

We were there to witness a situation in which a very senior government executive met with a roomful of contractors engaged in implementing a number of IT platforms. The official made his desires clear.

> "Look, don't tell me that everything is proceeding according to requirements if they are not. There are things being put into motion way up the line, promises being made, based on whether we have this system in place and operational by this date. We've had meeting after meeting about why things aren't getting done, but no one is actually telling me that we are going to miss our end date. I need to know. Tell me the truth. Are we going to make our end date?"

Dead silence.

Although every single contractor knew there was a problem and knew that the end date was going to come and go without an operational system, no one was willing to speak up.

Why did this happen? Well, under the terms of the contract, as long as each contractor had fulfilled his or her technical obligations, there would be no blame attached, nor consequences imposed. If the system were late, the result would inevitably be a contract extension and quite probably additional funds.

In other words, this situation had a structural conflict between the needs and goals of the organization and the needs and goals of the contractors. This situation is hardly unique to government, but it brings up one of the most challenging long-term issues any BKPM can face: the question of motivation.

Have you ever met an unmotivated person? When we ask that question, every hand shoots up. But let's think differently for a minute. Have you ever met someone who spends more time and energy each day scheming to get out of the work than it would take to actually get it done? Most likely, your answer is yes. And if that's the case, then you have to admit that this person is actually quite motivated — just in the wrong direction.

When any BKPM confronts noncooperation, the most important skill is diagnosis. *If someone isn't doing what I want, why not?*

There are three fundamental reasons, as shown in Figure 9-3.

Figure 9-3. The Iron Laws of Human Motivation. When someone isn't performing as desired, you must understand why before taking effective action.

The Diagnostic Question: "Why is someone not doing what I want him or her to do?"

Possible reasons:

1. They **don't know** what I want.

   Solution: Communication

   A "don't know" situation isn't a motivation issue, but rather a communications issue. Make sure they understand what you want them to do. Are your directions clear? Has the importance been communicated?

2. They **can't do** what I want.

   Solution: Remove the obstacle

   A "can't do" situation isn't a motivation issue either. If someone *really* can't do what you want, it may be training, tools, or aptitude that stands in the way. You must diagnose the barrier and see if you can remove it. Sometimes that involves changing the person, but usually you don't have to go that far.

3. They **won't do** what I want.

   Solution: Change the incentives

   Only "won't do" situations are motivational in nature. Remember, people don't do what you *want*, but rather what you *reward*, and they tend not to do what you punish. If you have a "won't do" situation, modify the motivations to change the behavior.

The Motivation Question: Why won't someone do what I want him or her to do?

Possible reasons:

1. Performance is **punished**.

   Solution: Remove the punishment

   If doing a good job on an unpleasant assignment results in you getting all the unpleasant assignments, you've been *punished for performance*. The likely result is lower performance in the future. In addition, other people notice this, and their performance suffers as well. Identify any ways in which people receive a negative incentive for doing what you want, and change it. Perhaps you can't undo all the negative consequences, but you can at least add positive rewards to compensate.

2. Failure is **rewarded**.

Solution: Remove the reward

In the example above, failing to meet the due date means a contract extension and more money. Combined with the lack of penalty for missing the deadline, the motivation is all too obvious. As in the previous case, you must *undo the rewards for failure* if you can, or at least add negative consequences for failure or additional positive consequences for success.

3. Performance **doesn't matter**.

Solution: Establish incentives

When even outstanding performers get assignments that seem pointless, motivation naturally suffers. If you're supposed to file lengthy reports and as far as you can tell, no one reads them, those reports are likely to get short shrift. If you're told this is an emergency and you jump to it, only to find out that it was never an emergency, you feel as if you've wasted your time. No one likes pointless work. *If the work is indeed pointless, remove it. If there's a point but the performers can't see it, make sure they know about it.* As with the other two categories, consider adding rewards for performance or potential consequences for nonperformance.

Above all, it's critical to align the rewards and negative consequences of your team with the goals of the client and the organization. If people support the goals, they need to have their own incentives tied in. Inaction is *not* a BKPM principle. When motivation is at stake, you must act and act quickly.

When a Project Becomes an Initiative

Projects end, but some programs and initiatives are ongoing. Often, they resemble a project in superficial ways, but there are usually key differences that the BKPM must recognize and manage.

Unlike projects, initiatives are either ongoing or have an end so far in the future that it's almost the same thing. Unlike projects, initiatives don't always have defined end states, such as an internal "continuous improvement" program. Unlike projects, initiatives are made up of such large components that there isn't any such thing as a single discrete process that leads from start to finish.

Apollo 11 was a project. Apollo itself was a program, consisting of multiple projects. The Kennedy-inspired mission to "landing man on the moon and returning him safely to this earth," on the other hand, was an initiative, driven at the highest organizational levels. Initiatives are by their nature tied deeply into overall organizational strategy. They are almost always very political, affecting numerous interests and careers.

Within the space program, there were many BKPMs. Earlier, we discussed mission director Gene Kranz, but he was far from the only leader. But the space program itself was led not by an astronaut, not by an engineer, not by the administrator of NASA, but by the then-Vice President of the United States, Lyndon Johnson. It was Lyndon Johnson who first drew Senate attention to the Soviet Sputnik launch, and in the process coined the phrase "space race." When he became President, John F. Kennedy put Lyndon Johnson in personal charge of the space program, and when he became President after Kennedy's assassination, Johnson continued to make the space program a top priority.

Lyndon Johnson was by any fair standard, bare-knuckled, but he wasn't a project manager as such. He was an executive politician, one of the most skilled practitioners in American history.

While BKPM principles can drive the process, it's even more important for the BKPM to keep the separation between owning the process and owning the outcome. A smaller focus — an Apollo mission, the Saturn V booster, the flight simulator program — is where the BKPM excels.

Watch also for large, complex, and amorphous initiatives in which there's no opportunity to tame the process or deliverables. Hurricane Katrina was the cause of the worst civil engineering disaster in United States history. Among the casualties were FEMA director Michael "You're doing a heckuva job" Brown and New Orleans Police Superintendent Eddie Compass, both of whom lost their jobs. The U. S. Army Corps of Engineers was assigned direct blame for the levee system failures, but escaped responsibility under the sovereign immunity doctrine.

There were successes in Katrina. The United States Coast Guard, the National Hurricane Center, and the National Weather Service were all commended for their actions before, during, and after the incident. But no matter how well they performed, the overall initiative can only be classified as a tragic disaster.

Success for the BKPM and success for the initiative aren't always the same thing. It's absolutely the case that the BKPM does everything possible to save the overall initiative, but when that isn't possible, the BKPM delivers excellence in whatever arena he or she can control.

The OODA Loop

A decision, Fletcher Knebel wrote, is something a man makes when he can't find anybody to serve on a committee. Of course, the BKPM can't afford to take that attitude. We must decide, and we must own our decisions.

United States Air Force Colonel (and BKPM) John Boyd developed a powerful decision-making model known as the OODA Loop (Observe, Orient, Decide, and Act), shown in Figure 9-4. Although it was originally designed for combat operations, it's gained increasing use in commercial operations and process management.

Figure 9-4. The OODA Loop. Observe, Orient, Decide, & Act.

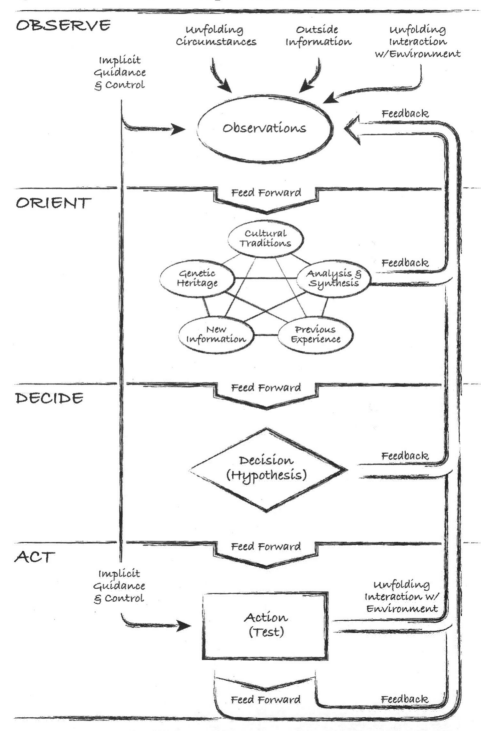

The decision-making process is a recurring cycle. The more rapidly and the more effectively you process this cycle, the better your decisions are likely to be.

The first step of the process is to **observe**. What are the circumstances around you? What are the environmental conditions? Is there outside information available? How have previous decisions been working out? What controls or constraints limit your range of action?

Next, it's vital to **orient** yourself. As Boyd himself wrote, "The second O, orientation – as the repository of our genetic heritage, cultural tradition, and previous experiences – is the most important part of the O-O-D-A loop since it shapes the way we observe, the way we decide, the way we act." Decisions often get stuck in this stage, especially when there are multiple actors in the process. After each participant applies his or own filters to the issue, there may be nothing else. The BKPM must break through the cycle powerfully but accurately. This involves understanding our own basic assumptions and attitudes, and learning how to correct for our internal biases.

The third step is to **decide**. A decision is in many ways a hypothesis, because it's uncertain. If the situation is complex, have you threaded your way through all the tradeoffs? Are you clear about what you want the decision to accomplish? Are you willing to accept the downside risks or negative side effects?

A decision by itself accomplishes nothing. The BKPM must therefore act, implementing the decision and monitoring the effects. And that in turn leads us back to **observe**, restarting the OODA Loop for our changed situation.

This applies not only to decisions within a project, but it also brings us full circle to "recovering value." That's the "observe" stage for the next project.

10

Transforming the Project — and the Organization

The Road to Excellence

Most PROJECTS, as we've seen, fail, and that's a terrible problem for most organizations. Projects are often our most important product. Projects are the way change takes place. Projects are the way problems get solved. Projects are the way we expand our business reach. Projects are the way we grow and prosper. When projects fail, the organization fails along with it.

The projects you choose, the resources you provide, and above all, the leadership you show make the critical difference between success and failure. Projects fail for many reasons, but the most important reason is lack of leadership.

Project leadership isn't the same thing as ordinary organizational leadership. Projects are temporary, which means that most project teams are temporary as well. Team members usually have permanent homes in other departments or other companies, along with supervisors, regular job requirements, and everything else that comes with the territory.

And those permanent supervisors are usually not the same people as the project manager. Project managers are temporary, part-time bosses with limited control over their team members. Project managers often can't fire people (though they can kick them off the team), or even discipline them officially.

In some ways, project managers are like the character Blanche DuBois in *A Streetcar Named Desire*, who famously said, "I have always depended on the kindness of strangers." We have all the responsibility, but usually not the official authority.

The Bare-Knuckled Project Manager understands that reality, but doesn't let it stand in the way. Leadership is far more than official supervisory authority. In fact, supervisory authority is usually not all it's cracked up to be. Just because someone is supposed to do what you say doesn't mean they actually will. Enabling great performance is the work of leaders. Ordinary project managers may be good enough for ordinary projects, but when the challenge is there, you need to "send for the sons of bitches."

Nothing matters more to your success than putting the right people in charge of it. No system, approach, method, or tool will deliver the results you need without the leadership of those in charge. That's why the essence of Bare-Knuckled Project Management is to find (or grow) Bare-Knuckled Project Managers who can get the job done.

The differences between a BKPM and a master project manager are key:

- The master project manager pursues career growth.
- The BKPM pursues results, and career growth follows.

- The master project manager pursues career stability.
- The BKPM pursues consistent results, and career demand follows.

- The master project manager pursues success.
- The BKPM pursues wins.

The Bare-Knuckled Customer

We've talked about the Bare-Knuckled Project Manager, but let's not forget the Bare-Knuckled Customer. Unlike project managers (of any sort), customers don't have to go through certification, learn a set of tools, or really much of anything else. The minimum qualifications of a customer are: (1) a need, and (2) the ability to pay. Everything else is optional.

While the job of the BKPM is to succeed regardless of the obstacles or challenges the customer, the organization, or the environment may provide, a great customer is a powerful asset in getting the job done. Through forced clarification and the three-sided table, the BKPM ensures that the customer is clear about desired outcomes, understands the risks and choices that need to be made, and is willing to make a commitment.

When a regular customer becomes a Bare-Knuckled Customer (BKC), he or she knows how to push the BKPM and the team for better results. The BKC knows what he or she wants, understands the costs and challenges perfectly, and demands the highest level of performance from the others at the three-sided table. The BKC understands where a hands-on approach is helpful, and where hands-off is better.

By understanding the overall bare-knuckled approach to project management, the BKC is an active, supporting partner in the drive for success.

The Bare-Knuckled Technical Team

Technical professionals are drawn from all walks of life, and bring their own unique perspectives to the job. Understanding the technical issues and challenges at stake, they make the detailed day-to-day decisions and choices that build the solution and deliver the desired outcome.

The danger with skilled technical professionals is that they'll dive down the rabbit hole of technical minutiae, spending disproportionate amounts of time and energy on minor issues, or even worse, push toward a technically elegant solution that isn't what the customer really wants or needs. That's why the BKPM isn't part of the solution team, but remains an independent part of the three-sided table.

Technical professionals, too, can take a bare-knuckled approach to the job. Bare-Knuckled Technical Professionals (BKTP) know how and when to push back. Sometimes the proposed solution is wrong-headed, or the customers and project managers have a completely unrealistic picture of what's involved. Work is like an iceberg: ninety percent of it is invisible to outsiders. That's why most jobs cost more and take longer than you think.

The first element that distinguishes the BKTP from an ordinary technical professional is *assertive communication*. The assertive part is the willingness to push back. A lot of technical professionals have that. It's the communications part where they often fall short. Each technical discipline has its own language, and it's often not the same language the customer speaks. (It may not always be the same language the BKPM speaks.) A true BKTP knows how to translate and convey the real issues in a way that project manager and customer can understand.

The second element that distinguishes the BKTP is *perspective.* It's easy to know your own field and your own issues. It's much more challenging to learn to see the world as others see it. The better you understand the issues and concerns of the customer and the project manager, the more effective you'll be in coming up with meaningful, useful solutions.

The third element of a BKTP is *positive energy.* While empty happy talk benefits no one, the technical professional who's a reliable wet blanket (and we all know who we're talking about) loses credibility and effectiveness at a rapid rate. Positive energy is contagious. It makes people more willing to listen. It drives the people around you to higher levels of achievement.

Perhaps most importantly, if you're known as a positive team player in general, you'll be listened to on the occasions when you have to deliver very negative news. That's something worth cultivating.

The Bare-Knuckled Organization

Some BKPMs are outside hired guns, brought in to fix troubled projects or to provide special skills. Other BKPMs are internal, whether they head the PMO or serve in an executive role overseeing the largest and toughest projects. Either way, organizational support is a crucial element that allows the job to get done.

As we've seen, it's primarily the responsibility of the BKPM to ensure that this support takes place. Through the three-sided table, the BKPM pushes the customer organization to face the reality of the project — to put up or shut up. That's vital for any project, but the organization can think and act better if it takes on a bare-knuckled identity of its own.

Bare-knuckled organizations recruit, develop, and promote bare-knuckled team members. Using limbic learning as a career development strategy, they develop BKPMs and help develop similar skills in line customers and technical teams as well.

Bare-knuckled organizations develop meaningful strategic and tactical visions. They know where they want to go and what it will take to get it there. They face the tough choices and hard decisions without self-imposed blinders. They clearly articulate what they want so that BKPMs, line customers, and team members understand what they have to do.

Bare-knuckled organizations aren't afraid of pushback — they welcome it. They're always willing to hear unpleasant news without shooting the messenger, and understand that fixing problems is more important than assigning blame.

Bare-knuckled organizations grow. By developing maturity in others, they grow in maturity themselves.

Bare-knuckled organizations succeed.

The Real World

Being a bare-knuckled project manager, a bare-knuckled customer, a bare-knuckled team member, or a bare-knuckled organization is a journey, not a destination. We can't get there overnight, and no matter how well we perform today, we're capable of performing even better tomorrow.

No matter how hard we try, none of us will achieve perfection. That means the BKPM always and necessarily swims in shark-filled waters. We have to train, counsel, and push our customers. We push team members to and beyond their limits. We challenge organizational assumptions and ways of doing business.

You can't be willing to tell the Emperor he has no clothes if you're desperate to keep your job. The BKPM has to put the customer's needs ahead of the customer's point of view, and that means giving people unpopular and unpleasant news.

What appears to be risking career suicide, however, is actually good for us as well. Too many people think you have to choose between being ethical and being successful, but we're convinced that's completely backward. Being strongly ethical *improves* your chances of success. People who have integrity and competence are always in demand — if not right here and right now, then somewhere else and soon.

In fact, the opposite is true. People who put their ethics on hold to do what the boss says may get short-term praise, but they're the first to be thrown to the wolves when the sled needs to be lightened.

In other words, for a BKPM, our jobs are in jeopardy when all we do is our jobs.

A Way of Life

Being bare-knuckled isn't just about running successful projects. A bare-knuckled approach is, as far as we're concerned, the best way to live our lives. Who wants empty safety and useless accomplishments when we can achieve greatness? Taking smart risks and putting ourselves on the line is the path to work that we take pride in, for achievements we can point to, for successes we helped bring into being.

In his famous speech on taking command of the United States Third Army, General George Patton defined for all times what it means to be bare-knuckled.

> "There is one great thing that you men will all be able to say after this war is over and you are home once again. You may be thankful that twenty years from now when you are sitting by the fireplace with your

grandson on your knee and he asks you what you did in the great World War II, you won't have to cough, shift him to the other knee and say, 'Well, your granddaddy shoveled shit in Louisiana.' No, sir, you can look him straight in the eye and say, 'Son, your granddaddy rode with the great Third Army and a son-of-a-goddamned-bitch named Georgie Patton!"

A project is ultimately about the destination, but the journey matters as well. Bare-Knuckled Project Managers get the job done. It is, after all, their *raison d'être*. But BKPMs also make the journey itself interesting, challenging, and fun. It's great to be a BKPM, and it's great to work for or with one as well.

At the beginning of this book, we invited you to call us so that you can experience first-hand what it means to have a BKPM at the helm of your project. Now that you know what a BKPM is, and how BKPMs work, we hope you'll take us up on that invitation.

Thanks for reading. We look forward to hearing from you.

General George S. Patton

Glossary

Access (Escape) Portals. A strategy the BKPM builds into the plan to allow bridging the gap with the customer when conflicts and problems arise. Access portals include agreeing about areas of relative flexibility, agreeing about responses to foreseeable risks, agreeing about approaches to unforeseeable risks and issues, and agreeing about processes for conflict resolution.

Agile. A method of software development that uses an iterative process with multiple cycles to bring the final product ever closer to the goal. Contrast with waterfall.

BKPM. Bare-Knuckled Project Manager, or alternately Bare-Knuckled Project Management. You can also have Bare-Knuckled Customers, Bare-Knuckled Technical Professionals, and even a Bare-Knuckled Organization.

Co-Opt Risk. What happens when the three-sided table breaks down and the project manager becomes aligned with one of the remaining two sides.

Driver. The leg of the Triple Constraint that cannot fail without bringing down the whole project.

Forced Clarification. The process by which the BKPM ensures that the customer or sponsor defines the outcome, a necessary precondition to moving forward with the project.

G-R-E-A-T. An acronym for team building, which works best when people are clear about goals, roles, expectations, attitudes and aptitudes, and time.

Iterative Approach. When the outcome isn't clear up front, the project may go through cycles and multiple prototypes to gain increasing clarity and understanding. May be part of an agile process.

Jeet Kune Do. A martial arts "style of no style" developed by Bruce Lee, and a metaphor for the BKPM approach.

Middle Constraint. The Triple Constraint that falls between the driver and the weak constraint.

PMBOK®. A PMI publication, short for *A Guide to the Project Management Body of Knowledge*, that provides a widely accepted standard for the practice of project management.

PMI. The Project Management Institute, a leading association of project managers.

PMO. Project Management Office, a division inside the organization that provides services, direction and support to the range of multiple projects that are taking place.

PMP®. Project Management Professional, a certification for project managers offered by PMI.

Recovering Value. The BKPM alternative to ineffective "lessons learned," a strategy to extract value from the project experience and results to benefit the organization and future projects.

S-M-A-R-T-(E-R). An acronym to measure whether a project objective is sufficiently detailed and clear: specific, measurable, agreed upon, realistic, time constrained, ethical, and rewarded.

Three-Sided Table. A BKPM approach to project management in which the BKPM owns the process (but not the outcome), the sponsor or customer owns the outcome (but not the process), and the partners and team own the technical solution.

Triple Constraint. The traditional set of constraints that shapes the world of any project, consisting of the time constraint, the cost (or resource) constraint, and the mandatory performance criteria, ranked in the order of flexibility as driver, middle constraint, and weak constraint.

Waterfall. What agile practitioners call conventional project planning, in which tasks have clear beginnings, endings, and dependencies.

Weak Constraint. The Triple Constraint that has the greatest flexibility.

Winston Wolf. A character in the film *Pulp Fiction*, used here as a metaphor for the BKPM in action.

Work Breakdown Structure (WBS). A method of breaking a project down into its component work packages, usually portrayed as an "organization chart" of the project work.

Bibliography

————— , *A Guide to the Project Management Body of Knowledge (PMBOK® Guide)*, 3rd Edition, Newtown Square, Pennsylvania: Project Management Institute, 2004.

Calleam Consulting, Ltd., "Catalog of Catastrophe," *Why Technology Projects Fail: A ResourceA Resource Center for Advanced Learning* (website), 2012: http://calleam.com/ WTPF/?page_id=3#2011, retrieved August 13, 2012.

Cialdini, Robert B. Ph.D., *Influence: The Psychology of Persuasion* (revised edition), New York: Quill (William Morrow), 1991.

Dobson, Michael, *Random Jottings 6: An Encyclopedia of Cognitive Bias*, Bethesda, Maryland: The Institute for Sidewise Thinking, 2011. (Free download at http://efanzines.com/ RandomJottings/RandomJottings06.pdf).

Dobson, Michael and Heidi Feickert, *The Six Dimensions of Project Management: Turning Constraints Into Resources*, Vienna, Virginia: Management Concepts, 2007.

Fisher, Roger, and William Ury, *Getting to Yes: Negotiating Agreement Without Giving In*, New York: Penguin, 1981.

Hartley, Gregory, and Maryann Karinch, *How to Spot a Liar: Why People Don't Tell the Truth and How You Can Catch Them* (revised edition), Pompton Plains, New Jersey: Career Press, 2012.

Sinek, Simon, *Start With Why: How Great Leaders Inspire Everyone to Take Action*, New York: Portfolio/Penguin, 2009.

The Standish Group International, Inc., *CHAOS Summary 2009: The 10 Laws of CHAOS*, Boston, MA: Standish Group, 2009.

Sun Tzu (孫子), *The Art of War*, (trans: Lionel Giles, 1910), Project Gutenberg edition (e-book).

Tarantino, Quentin and Roger Avary, *Pulp Fiction* (screenplay), New York: Miramax Films, 1994. Script retrieved from http://screenplayexplorer.com/wp-content/scripts/Pulp-Fiction.pdf, August 29, 2012.

Wasser, Alan, "LBJ's Space Race: What We Didn't Know Then (Part 1)," *The Space Review* (online journal), June 20, 2005. Retrieved from http://www.thespacereview.com/article/396/1, September 10, 2012.

Photo and Image Credits

The cover art and all original illustrations for this book were created by Bartley Collart working under his company name, L10. Bart's website is at www.L10.biz. He can be reached at bcollart@L10.biz, or (703) 879-1833.

Cover and back cover photographs were taken by Nick Gruebl.

All other photographs are from Wikimedia Commons or the Library of Congress Prints and Photographs Division, and are either in the public domain or are otherwise free for use.

John L. Sullivan Cigarette Advertising Card produced by Allen and Ginters, 1870s-1890s. (http://commons.wikimedia.org/wiki/File:John_L._Sullivan1.jpg). Public domain; copyright expired.

John L. Sullivan image in Figure 2-1: From a Currier & Ives print from the Library of Congress Prints and Photographs Division. Public domain; copyright expired. (http://www.loc.gov/pictures/item/90710653/)

Jeet Kune Do symbol, copyright © and trademark ® by Bruce Lee Estate. Per Wikimedia Commons, "The copyright holder of this work allows anyone to use it for any purpose including unrestricted redistribution, commercial use, and modification." (http://commons.wikimedia.org/wiki/File:Simbolo_JKD.jpg)

Gas metal arc welding. Photograph in the public domain because it was taken by a U.S. Air Force employee during the course of his or her official duties. Photo credit: USAF 040112-F-1663P-001. (http://commons.wikimedia.org/wiki/File:GMAW.welding.af.ncs.jpg)

Apollo 11 Crew: Official NASA photograph, not protected by copyright. (http://commons.wikimedia.org/wiki/File:The_Apollo_11_Prime_Crew_-_GPN-2000-001164.jpg)

Portrait of Apollo 1 astronauts praying. Official NASA photograph, not subject to copyright. (http://commons.wikimedia.org/wiki/File:A1prayer.jpg)

Mission Control celebrates successful splashdown of Apollo 13. Official NASA photograph, not subject to copyright. (http://commons.wikimedia.org/wiki/File:Mission_Control_celebrates_successful_splashdown_of_Apollo_13.jpg)

Portrait of George S. Patton by the U. S. Army, public domain. Original in the collection of the Library of Congress Prints and Photographs Division, Reproduction Number LC-USZ62-25122. (http://commons.wikimedia.org/wiki/File:GeorgeSPatton.jpg)

Acknowledgements

No book is ever the sole achievement of the listed authors, and this book is no exception. Thank you to those who encouraged us to take on this book as a project including (but not limited to) close family, Dana, Mom, Dad, Mel, Nick, Andy, John, Anibal, and Alexia; colleagues Bill Webster, Valerie, Kristy, Bryan and the team, Colin, Shawn, Jose, David, and Elizabeth; close customers Jeanne, Alix, and John D; and early influencers, Donna, Ralph, and Joe.

We drew inspiration from the work of authors George Gilder, John Eldredge, Randy Alcorn, Greg Hartley, Maryann Karinch, and Simon Sinek.

Many thanks to Nick at NGIP for the cover and author photographs for BKPM as well as to Valerie Smith and Bryan Wolbert for agreeing to let us use their images for the cover of this book. Valerie is Chief Administrative Officer, Vice President, and an active project manager for Think. Bryan is Executive Vice President, Chief Operating Officer, and a Sr. Project Manager. They are true representatives of Bare-Knuckled PM and practice the art every day. Thanks to Linda Mann for proofreading.

Our special thanks to those who awaken the sleepers and free the shackled in private and business life.

As always, any errors and omissions are ours alone.

Tony
Gruebl

Jeff
Welch

About the Authors

Tony Gruebl is a Six Sigma Master Black Belt and president of Think Systems, Inc. (Think), a technology project management and business intelligence (BI) consulting company he started in 2004.

His experience includes an extensive list of BI technology implementations and strategic project management and control engagements for domestic, international, and multinational firms over a twenty-year span.

In 2007, he led a series of technology implementations for a partner company that resulted in his team winning the AT&T Supplier Recognition Award in Customer Service from among 5,000 suppliers (as noted in the *Wall Street Journal* and Yahoo Finance on 6/5/07).

Before starting Think, Tony was the Chief Operating Officer of a Washington, DC, non-profit firm that is also one of the company's current clients.

This follows a career built in the Business Intelligence technology space, in which he served as vice president of a Pennsylvania-based OLAP financial software provider and Director of Consulting for a Bethesda, Maryland-based IT company specializing in focused solutions for the federal government.

Tony earned an MBA in Financial Management and Technology Entrepreneurship from Rensselaer Polytechnic Institute, studied abroad at the Copenhagen Business School, and completed his undergraduate work at Towson University. He lives in Perry Hall, Maryland, with his wife, Dana, and their four children and loves motorcycles and clinging to his God and guns.

Jeff Welch is a technical executive who specializes in the use of technology to deploy training, simulations, and performance-enhancing information systems throughout commercial, DoD, and civilian Government markets.

He is a program/project manager and solution architect with twenty-three years of broad-based expertise in systems development. While being highly technically oriented, he is also a proficient Instructional Systems Designer and instructor/speaker. Jeff relates to customers, stakeholders, and team members at executive through developer levels. He drives vision and business practices to maintain a top-line focus while balancing the operational needs of the projects he is leading.

Jeff is a proven problem solver and has a natural ability to motivate staff through unique challenges. He is also known for his ability to write and present highly technical concepts and project plans in a manner that non-technical stakeholders can understand and is often called upon to provide a liaison between technology-based services and other business units (e.g., executive stakeholders, operations managers, designers, and developers).

Outside of the workplace, Jeff is an eclectic personality who has many interests and hobbies. He is a private pilot, enjoys whitewater kayaking, and is an avid homebrewer who invents his own brewing equipment and recipes. He supports his son's motocross and daughter's equestrian activities and is the loving husband to his wife, Shelby, of more than twenty years.

Think Systems was formed in 2004 as a provider of project management, process improvement, solution design, and software implementation and customization services and for large and small companies. What we really love to do is solve business problems and own difficult projects, particularly in the technology space. We provide strategic and tactical project management, project control, PMO support, business analysis, and technical support as needed.

Bryan Wolbert and Valerie Smith are also principals of the firm. Bryan is Executive Vice President and COO and brings 15 years of business analysis and project management capability and he has been a volunteer firefighter for over 20 years. Valerie is Vice President and Chief Administrative Officer of Think where she manages the infrastructure of the company for our team while simultaneously running a large cornerstone project for one of our partners.

The company name, "Think Systems," is derived from the practice of systematizing business methods, people, and their efforts in order to achieve successful software implementation outcomes. We architect and own the processes to achieve the outcomes that our customers envision.

Every implementation requires paying special attention to the embedded business processes and new ones created by adopting new software and creating workable solutions. And, since we are usually engaged to own the project management process, we focus tirelessly on risk management. Properly managing risk in a changing environment and "thinking about systems" in this way, rather than just installing software or simply checking off project management tasks, has resulted in implementation success for our customers and business success for Think Systems.

Think Systems, Inc., is headquartered in Baltimore, Maryland.

The authors may be reached through Think Systems, Inc. at www.thinksi.com, or 443-725-5131.

THINK SYSTEMS, INC.

9103 Gardenia Road
Nottingham, Maryland
21236-1766

T 443.725.5131
F 443.725.5132

www.thinksi.com

54291968R00125